What's This

got to do with anything?

Jim Craigen & Chris Ward

Kagan

Kagan Publishing
1160 Calle Cordillera
San Clemente, CA 92673
1(800) 933-2667
www.KaganOnline.com

ISBN: 1-879097-79-6

This book is dedicated to

Norm Green, whose tireless efforts on behalf of Co-operative Learning have inspired and energized us and to....

Barrie Bennett, our teacher, mentor and advocate, who has supported and sustained our professional growth.

Acknowledgements

We wish to acknowledge the support of Chuck Powers, Doug Wilson and Carol Yeo, Supervisory Officers of the Durham Board, for providing us with the many opportunities to do what we love to do — work with teachers for the betterment of kids through Co-operative Learning.

We especially wish to thank those teachers from the Durham Board and those from boards of education throughout Ontario and the United States who have attended our Co-operative Learning Institutes. Their encouragement and contributions provided the catalyst and many of the ideas that enabled us to get this book from the planning stage to print.

Chris and Jim

This book is a collection of tried and true activities which promote building the co-operative classroom.

We realize that a number of these have been around for years in many different shapes, forms, and variations. They represent what good teachers have been using to build positive environments conducive to learning.

Because many of these submissions come from a variety of teachers in and beyond the Durham Region, we have had no control over their source. If, by chance, an activity has been taken from a source, other than the public domain, this has not been intentional.

We welcome information that would enable us to cite and credit sources.

This collection is a direct result of our belief in the power of group and class building. It is our firm notion that in order for Co-operative Learning to be successful, it must take place in an atmosphere of mutual support that promotes risk taking and sharing.

After many years of employing Co-operative Learning with students and with teacher groups, we have developed a strong conviction that teachers cannot effectively utilize Co-operative Learning structures unless time and energy have been taken to build a solid foundation of trust. In our opinion, this is best done through the use of interactive activities that promote and sustain team building.

Whatever the length of our workshop presentations on Co-operative Learning (from one hour to one week) we ensure that adequate time is spent on contact activities that promote getting acquainted, allow for group formation and team building as well as providing energizing breaks to help us all refocus. Sometimes these are content-driven, sometimes they are purely "fun".

Invariably, someone, who is eager to get to "the meat" of the presentation approaches us and asks "What's this got to do with anything?" It is only as the session progresses that these same people begin to see the power of these activities in establishing a cohesive group and a secure environment.
Hence – the name of our book.

We hope that you will use these activities on a continuous basis to build and sustain powerful teams within your own caring, co-operative classroom.

Chris and Jim

How to Use This Book

When we examined the hundreds of activities that we collected we had to determine how best to categorize them. We decided on the following four categories:

- **Getting Acquainted**
- **Group Formation**
- **Group/Class Building**
- **Energizers**

These categories seemed to fit the kinds of activities that we deemed important in developing the co-operative classroom.

Some of the activities can be used in more than one category. Don't let our categorization hinder your use - apply them wherever you wish.

We have also identified the target audience by four divisions which are:

- **Primary**   (Grades K - 3)
- **Junior**   (Grades 4 - 6)
- **Intermediate**   (Grades 7 - 10)
- **Senior**   (Grades 11 - adult)

You will find the four categories of activities listed according to the following divisions:

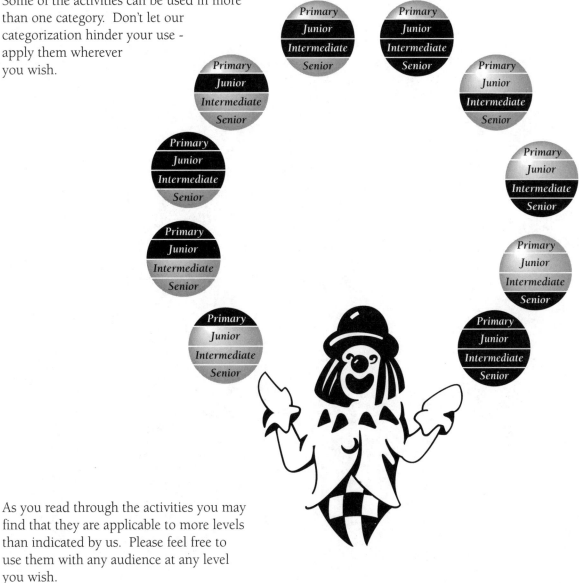

As you read through the activities you may find that they are applicable to more levels than indicated by us. Please feel free to use them with any audience at any level you wish.

Table of Contents

Table of Contents

Table of Contents

Table of Contents

Getting Acquainted

Choo Choo

Primary
Junior
Intermediate
Senior

Group Size: 10+

Time Line: 5 minutes maximum

Equipment Needed: none

Space Required: enough room to form a circle with all group members

Activity Description:

1. One person is the "conductor" in the centre of the circle.
2. He/she moves around the inside of the circle saying "choo choo choo ..." and stops at someone in the circle (person 2).
   Conductor: Hi, I'm Elissa. What's your name?
   Person 2: Hi, Elissa. My name is Helen.
   Conductor: Helen! Helen! Helen! Helen! Helen! Reverse!
3. The conductor then rotates (180°) so that person 2 is behind her.
4. Person 2 holds onto the conductor's waist to form a train.
5. The train continues to find the next person. At the next person,
   Conductor: Hi ... What's your name?
   Person 3: ... Catherine.
   Conductor: (passes it on to all members of train) Catherine!
   Person 2: Catherine!
   train together: Catherine! Catherine! Catherine! Catherine! Catherine! Reverse!
6. Everyone reverse. Person 3 is at end of train and now person 2 (was at end) is at front so she is the conductor. Continue.

What's This Got To Do With Anything • Jim Craigen & Chris Ward
Kagan Publishing • 1 (800) 933-2667 • www.KaganOnline.com

3

Name Tag Activity

Primary
Junior
Intermediate
Senior

Group Size: whole class

Time Line: 15-20 minutes

Equipment Needed: name tags

Space Required: any part of the room where you can gather the kids into a circle

'Frog'

Activity Description:

1. This is done at the beginning of the year. Children gather at the reading circle for the morning opening.
2. Teacher distributes name tags at random so students do not have their own.
3. We play music/sing a song or clap a rhythm and when we stop, one person is chosen to read the name tag he/she has.
4. He/she then must find the person who belongs to the name tag.

Variation:
Do it like concentration. Teacher lays out the tags in random order. Students study them for several minutes and turn them over. Each child takes a turn and must remember where he/she saw his/her name. Tags must be seen and turned over more often when using this approach.

Getting To Know You

Primary
Junior
Intermediate
Senior

Group Size: group 5-10

Time Line: until finished

Equipment Needed: nothing

Space Required: circle

Activity Description:

1. Person #1 says name, e.g. Jim and an occupation that begins with first letter of name, e.g. juggler.
2. Next person says first person's name, occupation (Jim-juggler), plus one for themself (Lisa-librarian).
3. Next person repeats first and second, plus their own (Bill-barber).
4. Continue around circle.
5. Last person must recite all of them.

4

Alphabet Game

Group Size: can be large or small

Time Line: open

Equipment Needed: students, alphabet cards

Space Required: fairly large room

Activity Description:

1. Alphabet cards are placed on the wall in random order.
2. They should be spaced a bit apart.
3. Students gather in front of cards that begin with the first letter of first name.
4. They then introduce themselves.

Name Game

Group Size: 10+

Time Line: depends on size

Equipment Needed: none other than memory

Space Required: classroom

Activity Description:

1. Stand in circle.
2. First person states first name and something that they like that begins with the first letter of their name, i.e. "Bob likes bubble gum".
3. The second person is required to repeat what the first person said plus add his/her own.
4. The third person starts with person #1, #2 then adds own, etc.

What's This Got To Do With Anything • Jim Craigen & Chris Ward
Kagan Publishing • 1 (800) 933-2667 • www.KaganOnline.com

5

Fast Food Friends

Group Size: whole class

Time Line: 15 minutes

Equipment Needed: 1/2 pieces of lined paper (one per participant), pencils

Space Required: classroom

Activity Description:

1. On one side of a piece of paper, write 5 of your favourite foods (1 minute).
2. When you have completed your list, find at least 3 other people who like something on your list.
3. Find out each person's name and write it beside the food item s/he likes on your list (only one name for each food item).
4. Then find out each person's favourite place to eat and put that beside his/her name (the side not used by your food list). [Teacher notifies when one minute is left, and then tells when students should take their seats.]
5. When the teacher calls on student, he/she quickly picks one name from the list, tells who the person is and what he/she has found out about him/her.

[The person called upon describes one person; that person in turn describes another, and so on. No person is chosen twice. Any people not chosen will be chosen by teacher to quickly tell same type of information about themselves. Teacher ends by giving his/her own personal information.]

Know Your Neighbour

Group Size: any number in groups of 2

Time Line: 2-5 minutes

Equipment Needed: none

Space Required: small

Activity Description:

1. 2 people face each other.
2. Each has 1 minute to tell the other all they can about him/herself.
3. End of time, ask each to turn with backs to each other.
4. Then ask - colour of eyes, is she wearing earrings, etc.

What's This Got To Do With Anything • Jim Craigen & Chris Ward
Kagan Publishing • 1 (800) 933-2667 • www.KaganOnline.com

Know Your Class

Group Size: 15-25

Time Line: 20-25 minutes

Equipment Needed: none

Space Required: enough space for one big circle

Activity Description:

1. Each person, in order, says his or her first name.
2. Then #2 says the name of #1, then #3 says names of #2 and #1, then #4 says names of #1, #2 and #3 until #25 says the previous 24 names.

Variations:
a) Start on the other side of the circle.
b) Switch number of positions and start again.

Bingo

Group Size: over 10 students

Time Line: varies, but could be about 5 minutes

Equipment Needed: Bingo sheet (see next page), pencil

Space Required: enough room for the group to move around in

Activity Description:

1. Sign student's name on page if desired.
2. Students put names of others who match them in that square.
3. When they have a straight line (or two straight lines) filled in, they yell, "Bingo".
4. They can each be rewarded as they finish, or numbered off for groups (i.e. 1, 2, 3, 1, 2, ...).

What's This Got To Do With Anything • Jim Craigen & Chris Ward
Kagan Publishing • 1 (800) 933-2667 • www.KaganOnline.com

People Bingo

Primary
Junior
Intermediate
Senior

same eye colour	same favourite sport	same class before now	same video game	same number of brothers
same number of sisters	same number of letters in first name	same colour of shoes	same city of birth	same favourite ice cream
same favourite colour	same number of aunts	FREE	same month of birth	same type of house
same favourite pop	same colour of hair	same favourite T.V. show	same favourite singing group	same favourite song
same pet	same bedtime	wearing same colour	same favourite movie	same height

What's This Got To Do With Anything • Jim Craigen & Chris Ward
Kagan Publishing • 1 (800) 933-2667 • www.KaganOnline.com

Personality Indicator

Group Size: unlimited

Time Line: 10 minutes

Equipment Needed: 1 pencil, 1 piece of paper for each participant

Space Required: participants working independently at their desks

Activity Description:

1. Participants choose their favourite colour and then describe it with 3 adjectives.
2. Choose their favourite animal and then describe it with 3 adjectives.
3. Choose their favourite body of water and then describe it with 3 adjectives.
4. Share information with small group or class.

Analysis:

1. descriptors of favourite colour describe how you see yourself
2. descriptors of favourite animal describe how others see you
3. descriptors of favourite body of water describe how you view nature

Make A Picture

Group Size: 30-35 students

Time Line: 15 minutes

Equipment Needed: magazine pictures - "busy" with lots going on

Space Required: full classroom

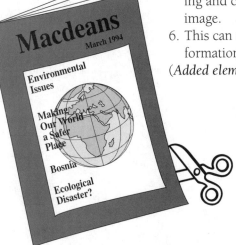

Activity Description:

1. Cut approximately 8 pictures from a magazine.
2. Cut each picture into 4 pieces.
3. Randomly distribute the pieces of each picture throughout the class (32 pieces).
4. Objective is to recreate the pictures.
5. Students move around room cooperating and communicating to create final image.
6. This can also be used for a group formation activity.
(*Added element* - give a time limit)

9

What's This Got To Do With Anything • Jim Craigen & Chris Ward
Kagan Publishing • 1 (800) 933-2667 • www.KaganOnline.com

Forced Choices

Primary
Junior
Intermediate
Senior

Group Size: whole class

Time Line: 30 minutes

Equipment Needed: pens and paper

Space Required: classroom

Activity Description:

1. Each person is asked to write an answer to the following questions.
   Are you: more of a saver or spender?
   loner or grouper?
   rose or daisy?
   breakfast or dinner?
   summer or winter?
   teacher or student?
   etc.
2. After making these decisions, write a description of the sort of person you might be.

Discussion:
Show your list to a partner. Ask him/her to say whether he/she agrees with you. Why? Why not?

Classmates

Primary
Junior
Intermediate
Senior

Group Size: whole class (whether 20 or 33)

Time Line: 30 minutes (or so)

Equipment Needed: pen and hand-out (see next page)

Space Required: whole classroom

Activity Description:

1. At the beginning of the year/semester, each student gets the handout and with a time limit of possibly 10-15 minutes must get up and circulate and question other students in order to fill out the "questionnaire".
2. After the 10-15 minutes, another 3 minutes is given to pair/share and then meet with another pair to compare answers (3 minutes).
3. Then we take up the questions as a class so that everyone can learn about everyone else.

10

Classmates

Primary
Junior
Intermediate
Senior

TALK WITH YOUR CLASSMATES TO FIND OUT SOMETHING ABOUT THEM, THEN ANSWER EACH OF THE FOLLOWING QUESTIONS.

1. How many girls are there in this class? _____

2. How many boys are there in this class? _____

3. Who has the most brothers? _____ How many? _____

4. Who has the most sisters? _____ How many? _____

5. Who is an only child? _____

6. Who is the tallest? _____ Height? _____

7. Who is the shortest? _____ Height? _____

8. Who has blonde hair? _____

9. Who has black hair? _____

10. Who has red hair? _____

11. Who wears glasses? _____

12. Who has played on a school volleyball team? _____

13. Who has blue eyes? _____

14. Who takes Physical Education this semester? _____

15. How many are left-handed? _____

16. Who has not always lived in this town/city/village? _____

17. Who lives the closest to the school? _____

18. Who lives the farthest from the school? _____

19. Who has travelled the farthest on a holiday this summer? _____

    Where? _____

20. Who plays a musical instrument and what type of instrument is it?

    _____

11

What's This Got To Do With Anything • Jim Craigen & Chris Ward
Kagan Publishing • 1 (800) 933-2667 • www.KaganOnline.com

Remembering Your Youth

Group Size: any group size

Time Line: 10-15 minutes

Equipment Needed: card or piece of paper divided into 4 sections

Space Required: classroom, cafeteria - adequate space for number of people

Activity Description:

1. Organize the large group into 3 or 4 groups of 6-9 people.
2. Each person takes a blank piece of paper and divides it into 4 sections.
3. Each person is to share an experience they can recall from their adolescent years or junior-high years.
4. After sharing with each other, the pair must initial or sign one of the squares. Each person must share with four people in their group and get them to sign.
5. Provides opportunity to meet new people and provides a springboard into adolescent experiences and discussions on developmental characteristics of early adolescence.

My Personality

Group Size: class divided into smaller groups

Time Line: 1 hour

Equipment Needed: various items, e.g: can opener, hair brush, umbrella, crayon box

Space Required: classroom (not too large and circle of chairs)

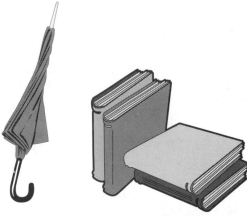

Activity Description:

1. Dump items on floor or table in centre.
2. Students all come up at once and choose an item about which they are willing to say "I am like this - because I ..." and "I am unlike this - because I ..." (Tell them previously what they'll be doing/saying with item.)
3. It is AMAZING how they reveal personality traits when comparing themselves to the item.
4. All group members get to know each other much better.

"I'm like this book because I like to tell stories."
"I'm not like this book because I don't like people to hold/touch me."

12

Journal Jottings

Group Size: whole class

Time Line: 5-10 minutes

Equipment Needed: pencils, stencils, journal

Space Required: classroom

Activity Description:

1. Each student begins with the stencil which he/she gets filled out by asking various others to fill in the blanks with wacky suggestions.
2. The students then go back to their desks and write up the information in a journal entry of 1 or 2 lines.
3. Students then share these wacky entries with the class.

Stencil suggestion on bottom.

first name _____

last name _____

profession _____

age _____

colour of hair and style _____

one adjective to describe this person _____

_____

another adjective to describe this person __

_____

Primary
Junior
Intermediate
Senior

What's This Got To Do With Anything • Jim Craigen & Chris Ward
Kagan Publishing • 1 (800) 933-2667 • www.KaganOnline.com

Same Birthday

Primary
Junior
Intermediate
Senior

Group Size: whole class

Time Line: 5 minutes

Equipment Needed: 30 chairs

Space Required: classroom

Activity Description:

1. Predict the number of duplicate days of birth.
2. Number each chair/desk - 1 to 31.
3. Students stand by the seat of their birth and find others with the same birthday and month.
4. Students can be numbered off to form new random groups for short term activities.

Getting Acquainted

Primary
Junior
Intermediate
Senior

Group Size: any size class over 15

Time Line: 10 minutes

Equipment Needed: Get Acquainted sheet, pencil or pen

Space Required: classroom

Activity Description:

1. See next page for record sheet.

What's This Got To Do With Anything • Jim Craigen & Chris Ward
Kagan Publishing • 1 (800) 933-2667 • www.KaganOnline.com

Getting Acquainted

GETTING ACQUAINTED SHEET

Names and faces go together soon after you have met your classmates. But you know very little about your friends if you know only their names.

Find out about your classmates by completing the blanks below with the names of your classmates. Try to find a different person for each description.

Find a classmate . . .

1. who has blue eyes _____

2. who has three brothers _____

3. whose middle name has six letters _____

4. who has travelled to another country _____

5. whose parent is a teacher _____

6. who is _____ centimetres tall _____

7. whose favourite TV show is the same as yours _____

8. who has gone to camp _____

9. who likes to read _____

10. who wears glasses _____

11. who likes spinach _____

12. whose favourite colour is purple _____

13. who has a birthday in September _____

14. whose father's name is Jim _____

15. who lives more than one km from school _____

16. who is the only child in the family _____

17. who rides a bus to school _____

18. who has a married sister _____

19. who is afraid of mice _____

20. who has two great-grandparents _____

Overtime: Make up other descriptions and find classmates who will fit the descriptions.

What's This Got To Do With Anything • Jim Craigen & Chris Ward
Kagan Publishing • 1 (800) 933-2667 • www.KaganOnline.com

Les commères - Did you know that ...?

Primary
Junior
Intermediate
Senior

Group Size: whole class

Time Line: beginning of the year

Equipment Needed: none

Space Required: classroom - sufficient space to form two lines

Activity Description:

1. Ask students to think of something that they wish to share about themselves. It should be something that no one knows but that you wish to share.
2. Have students form two lines (face to face).
3. Tell the person facing you the information you have chosen to share.
4. Students can now mingle in the group and tell someone else, etc.
5. The activity continues until the teacher says "freeze".
6. Teacher asks a few students to share what they learned about their classmates.

Scavenger Hunt

Primary
Junior
Intermediate
Senior

Group Size: 6 →

Time Line: 5 minutes (depends on number of people to find)

Equipment Needed: activity sheet, pen/pencil

Space Required: any room that can hold capacity of people involved in activity

Activity Description:

How much can you learn about the people in your group? This exercise will give you a chance to meet and find out something about your group members. You have two minutes to find and record the answers to each of these inquiries.

Find someone ...

1. who has travelled outside of Canada.
2. who has been living in their house for less than five years.
3. who can count to ten in another language.
4. who has gone skating/skiing this year.
5. who is planning to travel during March break.
6. etc.

What's This Got To Do With Anything • Jim Craigen & Chris Ward
Kagan Publishing • 1 (800) 933-2667 • www.KaganOnline.com

The Group Handshake

Group Size: ≤ 20

Time Line: 5 minutes

Equipment Needed: none

Space Required: standing room

Activity Description:

1. Assemble the group standing in no particular pattern.
2. Teacher introduces self to a student emphasizing the names of both parties.
3. Shake hands and don't release grip.
4. Teacher asks first student to introduce teacher to next student.
5. They shake but don't release grip.
6. #2 introduces #3 to #1.
7. #3 introduces #2 to #4.
8. All retain grasp.
9. Last person introduces second last to teacher to complete chain.
10. All names have been heard and group has enjoyed the activity.

Primary
Junior
Intermediate
Senior

Personal Possession

Group Size: small group or whole class

Time Line: dependent upon size of group

Equipment Needed: nothing special

Space Required: group space

Activity Description:

1. Each person in the group takes one "possession" on body or from wallet or brought into class at the time and tells the group why this is important to them or what it reveals about them.

   i.e - runners - athlete
   - ring - boyfriend
   - driver's licence - independence

Primary
Junior
Intermediate
Senior

What's This Got To Do With Anything • Jim Craigen & Chris Ward
Kagan Publishing • 1 (800) 933-2667 • www.KaganOnline.com

Spool of Thread Introduction Activity

Primary
Junior
Intermediate
Senior

Group Size: groups of 4-6

Time Line: 10-15 minutes

Equipment Needed: 1 spool of thread

Space Required: none

Activity Description:

1. Each member of the group tears off a piece of thread, any length.
2. One at a time, each person slowly winds the thread around his/her finger, while talking about himself/herself - the longer the thread, the more is disclosed about student's personal life and interests.

Memory Box

Primary
Junior
Intermediate
Senior

Group Size: small or large group

Time Line: can modify but generally 5-6 minutes

Equipment Needed: imagination, memory, paper/pencil for each person

Space Required: any space

Activity Description:

1. Ask people to pretend they have a shoe box in front of them.
2. Tell them to put 5 things (imagined) in the box that represents 'them'. (2 minutes) i.e. kids, hobby, wish, etc. - things that can fit in the box.
3. Now pair up with other person in group and share what's in the 'box'. (1 minute per person)
4. Tell pairs: "Now introduce each other to the group based on what you shared with each other."

Extension:
Have people take 1 item out of their box because their imaginary box has shrunk. (Keep it a secret!) At the end of the morning session give the partner a chance to figure out which of the 5 items their partner took out, knowing their partner more since they've worked together.

What's This Got To Do With Anything • Jim Craigen & Chris Ward
Kagan Publishing • 1 (800) 933-2667 • www.KaganOnline.com

Animal Cards

Group Size: any size

Time Line: 10 minutes

Equipment Needed: pins, cards with animal names

Space Required: open space to move

Activity Description:

1. Pin the animal name on the back of each student.
2. Students move around asking one question about their animal - yes or no questions.
3. When they have figured out their animal, pin on front.
4. One guess per question.

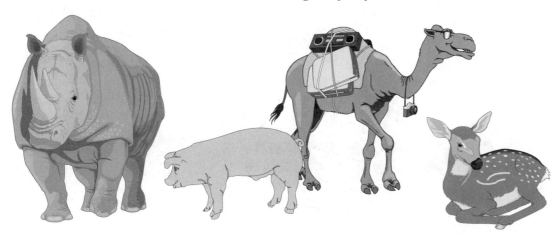

Back-to-Back

Group Size: full class

Time Line: 10-15 minutes

Equipment Needed: none

Space Required: may be done in regular class as long as fairly fluid movement is possible

Activity Description:

1. Teacher calls "back-to-back" after instructing everyone to find someone to back onto. The teacher also finds a partner if necessary to create an odd person.
2. The odd person left calls out "back-to-back" and everyone chooses a different back. Good for spatial awareness.

19

What's This Got To Do With Anything • Jim Craigen & Chris Ward
Kagan Publishing • 1 (800) 933-2667 • www.KaganOnline.com

Pulling Together or Pulling Apart

Group Size: two or more

Time Line: open

Equipment Needed: none

Space Required: classroom is fine

Activity Description:

1. To play this game, divide players into pairs.
2. Have each pair kneel face-to-face, hold onto each other's arms, and try to stand up, but first tell them to pull in opposite directions, then to push toward each other.
3. Also have each pair try standing from a sitting position back-to-back with only their palms touching.

Ball Toss

Group Size: whole class

Time Line: 10-15 minutes

Equipment Needed: up to 10 koosh balls or lightweight object (nerf ball, knotted socks)

Space Required: large circle

Activity Description:

1. This is a sequencing activity, an excellent mixer. (Persons have one hand up until they are selected; all will be selected).
2. Starter states "Mary, this is for you", tosses the ball to Mary, Mary answers, "Thank you, Paul".
3. Mary states "This is for you, Jessie, tosses the ball.
4. Jessie answers "Thank you, Mary".
5. This continues until all persons have been selected once.
6. The last person states, "This is for you, Paul" and tosses it to the starting person.
7. Paul thanks that person.
8. This is one complete revolution.
9. Paul will control the starting speed and the number of balls introduced.
10. Always the sender tosses to the same receiver.
11. It is a great way to learn names and energize!

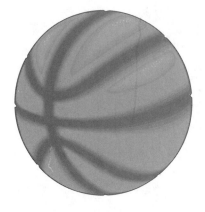

What's This Got To Do With Anything • Jim Craigen & Chris Ward
Kagan Publishing • 1 (800) 933-2667 • www.KaganOnline.com

Who Am I?

Group Size: 10-30

Time Line: 10 minutes

Equipment Needed: tags fixed to people's backs with famous fictional or non-fictional names

Space Required: room - no mirrors

Activity Description:

1. Students circulate with signs on backs.
2. Person cannot know whose name is on his/her back.
3. They may only ask each person they meet *one* yes or no question to discover who they are.

Guess What or Who?

Group Size: varies

Time Line: 10 minutes

Equipment Needed: cards with words or pictures, tape or pins (to attach cards)

Space Required: classroom size

Activity Description:

1. Each person gets a card put onto his/her back with a picture or word on it (gear to topic).
2. You can ask only yes/no questions - one per person being asked, then move onto another person and ask a yes/no question.
3. Try to discover what word is on your back.
4. Can be used to pair people (find your other half) or group people (if you are an animal then you are in that group, all colour words make a group, etc.).

21

Guess Who?

Primary
Junior
Intermediate
Senior

Group Size: class

Time Line: 10-15 minutes

Equipment Needed: index cards, masking tape, question sheet, pen/pencil

Space Required: classroom

Activity Description:

1. Write name on index card (cartoon character, movie star, body part).
2. Tape cards to forehead of students so that everyone may see what character they are.
3. With a question record sheet, the students are to mix and ask yes/no questions in order to deduce the character on their forehead.
4. They are to record the name of each person that they questioned.
5. Only one question per person.
6. If they figure it out quickly - have extra cards available.

Autographs

Primary
Junior
Intermediate
Senior

Group Size: any class size

Time Line: approximately 10 minutes

Equipment Needed: a sheet of paper with about 20 activities, preferences, likes, dislikes.

Space Required: classroom space is adequate

Activity Description:

1. Students receive an autograph sheet. (See next two pages as samples.)
2. In ten minutes, students must get others to sign their name beside an activity they do.
3. Students cannot write their name more than once on one sheet.
4. After ten minutes, have students hand sheets in. Share if desired.

What's This Got To Do With Anything • Jim Craigen & Chris Ward
Kagan Publishing • 1 (800) 933-2667 • www.KaganOnline.com

Autograph Sheet

Primary
Junior
Intermediate
Senior

Get as many different signatures from class members as possible.

1. likes to ski _____

2. can cook his/her own meals _____

3. has read a book by Judy Blume _____

4. saw "Honey, I Shrunk the Kids" _____

5. owns a Batman T-shirt _____

6. babysits _____

7. went to a cottage this summer _____

8. has journeyed outside Canada _____

9. is the eldest child in the family _____

10. plays the violin _____

11. wears size 7 shoes _____

12. has more than one pet _____

13. watches THE WONDER YEARS _____

14. likes old Beatles' music _____

15. has a younger brother _____

16. has lived somewhere other than Ontario _____

17. has had their tonsils removed _____

18. loves computers _____

19. lives in an apartment _____

20. wants to pursue a career in sports _____

21. has sung in a choir _____

22. can speak another language _____

23. likes peanut butter and banana sandwiches _____

24. has been camping _____

25. has been on a volleyball team _____

26. is a good artist _____

27. takes lessons outside school _____

28. has some difficulty in math _____

23

What's This Got To Do With Anything • Jim Craigen & Chris Ward
Kagan Publishing • 1 (800) 933-2667 • www.KaganOnline.com

Meeting People

Primary
Junior
Intermediate
Senior

Get the signature of a classmate who . . .

1. has a cat for a pet _____

2. has raised gerbils or hamsters _____

3. likes volleyball _____

4. wears size 5 shoes _____

5. has been to Disney World, Florida _____

6. owns a cottage _____

7. lives north of _____

8. watches the T.V. show _____   _____

9. listens to heavy metal _____

10. went to a live concert this summer _____

11. visited Canada's Wonderland _____

12. celebrated a birthday in the summer _____

13. likes pizza with anchovies _____

14. wears Nikes _____

15. loves the colour purple _____

16. saw the movie _____   _____

17. had cereal for breakfast this morning _____

18. has a part-time job _____

19. plays a musical instrument _____

20. has taken dancing lessons _____

21. plays hockey _____

22. has an older brother _____

23. has had their tonsils removed _____

What's This Got To Do With Anything • Jim Craigen & Chris Ward
Kagan Publishing • 1 (800) 933-2667 • www.KaganOnline.com

Autograph Descriptors

Primary
Junior
Intermediate
Senior

Group Size: any

Time Line: 10 minutes

Equipment Needed: worksheet,
  pen/pencil

Space Required: room

Activity Description:

1. Provide students with a list of 10-15 descriptors.
2. Have a space beside each for a name.
3. Students must collect autographs of those who fit the descriptor. (see bottom for examples)

1. Someone who thinks the Prime Minister is doing a good job. _____

2. Someone with my same astrological sign. _____

3. Someone who likes to work alone. _____

4. Someone who likes poetry. _____

5. Someone who loves dogs. _____

6. Someone from a large family. _____

7. Someone who plays a musical instrument. _____

8. Someone who works on the weekends. _____

9. Someone who prefers bikes to cars. _____

10. Someone who enjoys competition. _____

25

Name Bingo

Group Size: any class(es)

Time Line: 10 - ? (depending on size)

Equipment Needed: pencil

Space Required: classroom

Activity Description:

1. Place your name in the middle of bingo card and then introduce yourself to new students who will write their names on a space.
2. Then with class list in hand, play BINGO by calling out names of students.
3. Students complete their bingo cards.

Sci-Fi Bingo

Group Size: whole class

Time Line: flexible

Equipment Needed: copy of bingo card and pencil for each participant

Space Required: classroom

Activity Description:

1. Participants are required to find someone in group/class who fits each category on bingo card. All spaces must be filled. (See next page.)

- can be adapted to other topics

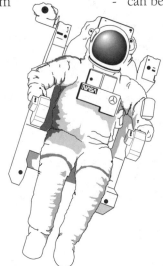

What's This Got To Do With Anything • Jim Craigen & Chris Ward
Kagan Publishing • 1 (800) 933-2667 • www.KaganOnline.com

Sci-Fi Bingo

Primary
Junior
Intermediate
Senior

I've seen an episode of STAR TREK or DR. WHO	I'd like to go on a space shuttle.	I own some science fiction books.	I have read a science fiction book by _____.	I think "The Iron Man" is an excellent book.
I have seen the movie, "20,000 Leagues Under the Sea."	I make delicious chocolate chip cookies.	I like to watch National Geographic specials on T.V.	I have visited the Kennedy Space Center in Florida.	I'd say that my favourite Star Trek character is _____ _____.
I've got friends who read science fiction books.	I saw the film, "The Empire Strikes Back."	FREE	I use a computer for word/data processing.	I know the year that man first walked on the moon.
I read science fiction articles in the newspapers	I own a personal computer.	I've read a book/story by either Isaac Asimov or Ray Bradbury.	I make a great lasagna.	I have heard of Buck Rogers.
I've read a book by Monica Hughes.	I've watched a shuttle take-off/landing on T.V.	I read "Discover" magazine in the library.	I'd like to try writing a science fiction story.	I think that Jules Verne was well before his time.

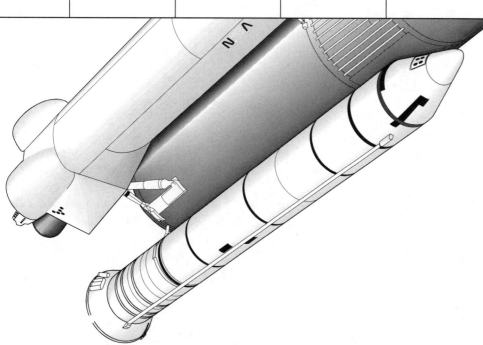

27

What's This Got To Do With Anything • Jim Craigen & Chris Ward
Kagan Publishing • 1 (800) 933-2667 • www.KaganOnline.com

My Favourite

Primary
Junior
Intermediate
Senior

Group Size: whole class

Time Line: 5 minutes (or longer)

Equipment Needed: pencils, paper

Space Required: classroom or areas of a classroom

Activity Description:

1. Each student writes his/her favourite under the following headings on his/her paper:
   1) Colour
   2) T.V. Show
   3) Activity/Game/Sport
2. Circulate and find 1 match with another person (i.e. same colour, T.V. show, etc.) - discuss all 3 areas.
3. Circulate and find another match with a new person and repeat above.
4. Switch every minute - new person/match - repeat above.

Snowball Fight

Primary
Junior
Intermediate
Senior

Group Size: class

Time Line: 10 minutes

Equipment Needed: white paper 8½" x 11" - one for each person, pen/pencil

Space Required: classroom - divide students in half and line them up on 2 opposite sides of room. You may want to move desks out of the way.

Activity Description:

1. Good for start of year, especially in a class where students have come from several "feeder" schools and don't know each other (i.e. grade 9).

2. Students are asked to print first and last name on sheet of paper.
3. Divide class in half and line students up facing each other on opposite sides of the room.
4. Crumple paper into a ball.
5. When teacher says *go*! throw the "snowball" at the students on the other side.
6. Pick up the snowballs on the floor, coming towards you, etc. and keep throwing them.
7. When teacher says *stop*! blows whistle, etc., find one snowball, undo it and find the person whose name is on it.
8. Introduce yourselves to each other, find out 3 interesting details about the person whose name you found.
9. Be prepared to introduce that person to the class and tell about them.

28

Group

Formation

WHAT'S THIS GOT TO DO WITH ANYTHING?

Let's Get Together

Primary
Junior
Intermediate
Senior

Group Size: regular class size

Time Line: 3-5 minutes

Equipment Needed: sets of pictures or word cards that go together, i.e. shoes and socks, cup and saucer, joystick and computer, etc.

Space Required: classroom

Activity Description:

1. Place cards face down on each desk.
2. Ring bell.
3. Students look at card and circulate to find "partner" and must then decide upon order. (i.e. cup and saucer not saucer and cup)
4. Partners stand together holding up picture plus one or two fingers to signal order.
5. This activity establishes random "pairs" for an activity. (The teacher may hand out the cards to ensure heterogeneous groupings if desired.)

Colour Match

Primary
Junior
Intermediate
Senior

Group Size: whole class

Time Line: 5-10 minutes

Equipment Needed: none

Space Required: corners or open areas of classroom

Activity Description:

1. Find someone with same colour (any article of clothing, hair, eyes, etc.).
2. Form groups according to whatever size teacher likes for group activity.

31

Colour Shapes

Primary
Junior
Intermediate
Senior

Group Size: multiples of 4

Time Line: 5-10 minutes

Equipment Needed: ▲ ● ■ ◆ shape cards in sets of different colours (1 colour per group of 4)

Space Required: classroom

Activity Description:

1. Each student is given one shape card (in one of the colours).
2. Objective is to find the other shapes in your sequence and in your colour (i.e. red ▲ must find red ●, red ■ and red ◆).

(Reinforces concept of colour and shape.)

Nursery Rhymes

Primary
Junior
Intermediate
Senior

Group Size: 4 in a group

Time Line: 5-10 minutes

Equipment Needed: 4 lines of a nursery rhyme cut in strips

Space Required: classroom

Activity Description:

1. Hand out nursery rhyme lines.
2. Find your rhyming partners.
3. Read the rhyme to whole group.

What's This Got To Do With Anything • Jim Craigen & Chris Ward
Kagan Publishing • 1 (800) 933-2667 • www.KaganOnline.com

Fly Around

Group Size: 20+

Time Line: 2-5 minutes (can be repeated)

Equipment Needed: none

Space Required: gym or classroom where areas are clear

Activity Description:

1. A divisible number of children are chosen to be "pilots". (e.g. 5 pilots for 20 children, 3 pilots for 18 - to make even groups)
2. Figure out how many groups you want - 1 pilot for each group.
3. Pilots sing "Fly around the (choose a topical word), e.g. "maple tree", "farm-yard".

   Fly around the maple tree
   Fly around the maple tree
   Fly around the maple tree
   Looking for a leaf.

   Rap and tap on someone's shoulder
   Rap and tap on someone's shoulder
   Rap and tap on someone's shoulder
   Now you've got a leaf. (partner)

4. Person whose shoulder is tapped joins pilot (behind), hands on waist.
5. Repeat verse and new person joins group, etc. until all children are chosen.

33

Sound Pairs

Primary
Junior
Intermediate
Senior

Group Size: any

Time Line: 10 minutes

Equipment Needed: double set of "sound" cards - "moo", "meow", "quack", etc.

Space Required: gym or classroom

Activity Description:

1. Divide class into 2 groups.
2. Sit one group in classroom.
3. Take other group to the hall.
4. Have each student in and out of classroom choose one card.
5. If possible, have lights turned out.
6. Have students from hall crawl in on hands and knees.
7. Have each student make their sound (in and out) and find their partner.

Match the Number

Primary
Junior
Intermediate
Senior

Group Size: any

Time Line: 15 minutes

Equipment Needed: number cards, number words and cards with number of stickers

Space Required: classroom

Activity Description:

1. Give each child a card.
2. They must match the number name, dots and figure.
3. When they are finished you have groups of three.

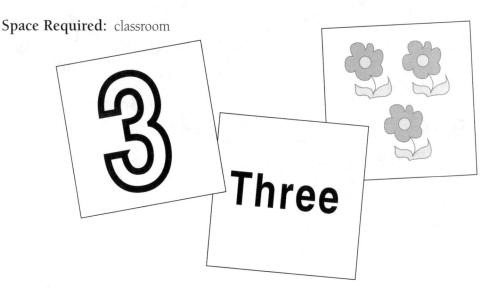

34

Toe-To-Toe

Primary
Junior
Intermediate
Senior

Group Size: any classroom size

Time Line: 3-5 minutes

Equipment Needed: gym (great for getting students into groups)

Space Required: gym or classroom area

Activity Description:

1. Students move around in gym and on the command "4 toe-to-toe" students must arrange themselves into a group of four and position themselves toe to toe.
2. Then the groups of fours could be used for games or gym lessons.
3. Other calls "2 knee-to-knee", "head-to-head", "nose-to-nose".

Students could also move with drama expression, move as proud ladies, old men, trees.

Animal Charades

Primary
Junior
Intermediate
Senior

Group Size: 24 (any number divisible by three)

Time Line: 5 minutes

Equipment Needed: cards with animal names or animal pictures (there must be 3 of each animal)

Space Required: classroom (you can use either a large cleared area or have students move around desks)

Activity Description:

1. Have students choose a card.
2. Without talking, using only sounds and gestures, each 'animal' must find their family. (i.e.: 3 lions, 3 dogs etc.)
3. Once a 'family' is found, the animals must share the sound or the gesture they used to represent their animal.

35

Decipher the Message!

Primary
Junior
Intermediate
Senior

Group Size: 3 groups of 8 (adjust according to class size)

Time Line: 3 minutes (approximately)

Equipment Needed: 3 colour coded sentences - with each word of sentence on separate paper (enough words in each sentence for one word/person)

Space Required: designate 3 open areas in classroom (in which 8 students can form a line)

ASOBNX 3Z52BANTCZX5CEHKHBANMILO
ROP3Z5BANT4R7XEF5Y6ASOBNX234BN
ASOBNX 9P28BANTCZX5CEHKABFNPANT
ASOBNX 3Z52BANTRHZ4CEHPSPFNSOS
ASOBNX6Q42BANTCZX5CEHKABFNLALA

Activity Description:

Teacher Preparation:
1. Each message is put on a different coloured paper.
2. Words of each message must be cut out.
3. Distribute one word to each student.

Activity:
1. Students find the members needed in their group according to colour.
2. Students sequence sentence in appropriate order in the time allotted.
3. When all groups have formed their sentence, they share their message with the other groups.

Barnyard Babble

Primary
Junior
Intermediate
Senior

Group Size: whole class activity, subgroups formed

Time Line: 5-10 minutes

Equipment Needed: none

Space Required: clear area in gym or class

Activity Description:

1. Generate a list of 5 or 6 barnyard animals.
2. Designate a corner or meeting place for each group.
3. Students pick their favourite animal from group and go to that area.
4. As a group, generate a call for your particular animal.
5. Spread out in open area.
6. Everyone closes eyes and finds his/her animal group using only the animal's call.

36

Compound Word Game

Group Size: whole class

Time Line: 5 minutes

Equipment Needed: 4 bowls (containers) any 2 different colours; i.e: 2 red - 2 blue; compound word cards divided in two, i.e. cow boy

Space Required: classroom

Activity Description:

1. Place a red word bowl and a blue word bowl together at one side of the room and a second pair at the other side.
2. Divide class into two teams.
3. Divide each team into two groups: the red word players and the blue word players.
4. Each of the red word players picks one word from his/her team's red word bowl and each of the blue word players picks a blue one.
5. The players try to find another member of their team whose word will combine with their own to form a compound word, e.g. up/stairs, marsh/mallow. (These players may be on the same side of the room or they may have to match to someone on the other side.)
6. When they have found their partner, each person talks about his or her word.

The Colour Game

Group Size: whole class divided into groups of four

Time Line: 1/2 hour

Equipment Needed: stickers, 4 baskets, list of items, coloured objects

Space Required: a variety of locations within the school

Activity Description:

1. Each student wears a coloured sticker.
2. Children group together according to sticker.
3. Each group is given a list of clues of objects it must find.
4. The common goal is that each item is the same colour as the group sticker.

What's This Got To Do With Anything • Jim Craigen & Chris Ward
Kagan Publishing • 1 (800) 933-2667 • www.KaganOnline.com

Create a Cartoon Story

Group Size: whole class divided into groups of 4

Time Line: 20-30 minutes

Equipment Needed: 1 large piece of paper (chart paper), glue, marker, pencil, 1 piece of scrap paper for each group and six cartoons of about 4 pictures each

Space Required: classroom

Activity Description:

1. Cut the cartoons into individual pictures.
2. Mix up the pictures and place them in a hat or bowl (folded).
3. Have each member of the class choose a picture and keep it hidden from the rest of the class.
4. Members of the class try to find other members with a picture that goes with their cartoon.
5. A group is formed from the members with pictures from the same cartoon.
6. Each group member is assigned a number that corresponds with a job such as materials gatherer, etc.
7. Each group will write a rough copy of a story to go with the cartoon.
8. The cartoon is pasted on the chart paper and the final story printed with marker.
9. Group presents story to rest of the class.

Match the Ad Pictures

Group Size: even number of participants (20-30)

Time Line: 20 minutes (approximately)

Equipment Needed: magazine ads - cut in 2 parts, pins or masking tape

Space Required: enough to move about

Activity Description:

1. Place all pictures on the backs of participants.
2. Players may ask questions to be answered Yes or No of any players as they attempt to match the other half of their ad.
3. Continue to repeat until everyone has been successful at finding a partner.

38

Word Train Chain Gang

Primary
Junior
Intermediate
Senior

Group Size: small groups of 4 (or whatever you wish)

Time Line: 7 minutes (more or less depending on level)

Equipment Needed: coloured strips of paper with one word printed on each (one for each student, 4 different colours), markers, glue stick

Space Required: classroom, desk clusters

Activity Description:

1. For establishing groups - strips may be handed out randomly, chosen in a draw, or assigned in order to separate potential problems.
2. In your hand you hold a strip of paper with one word printed on it.
3. Somewhere in this room are 3 other people whose words go with yours.
4. The first letter of your word may match the last letter of another word OR the last letter of your word may match the first letter of another word.
5. One word in each group will have no word-end to match at its beginning, and one word will have no word-beginning to match at its end.
6. Teacher may wish to draw a sample pat-

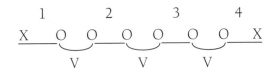

tern on the board to reinforce this.
(3 minutes to find)

7. When you have found all 4 words which fit together in this kind of pattern, write your name on your strip.
8. Number yourselves from 1-4 and put your number beside your name. (minute to complete)
9. The person with the number ___ will come and get a glue stick for your group. Glue your strips together in the right order to make a paper chain (demonstrate chain links).

Examples:
ball light tumble even
jelly yellow wink keep
bear red dim mash
clang golf forego ox
quagga areas stylus stash
buzz Zulu Urdu Uriah

39

Cooperative Captions

Primary
Junior
Intermediate
Senior

Group Size: whole class - 4 people per group

Time Line: first day of school (10-15 minutes)

Equipment Needed: calendar-size cartoons (captions removed) cut into 4 pieces jigsaw style, chart paper, glue stick, masking tape

Space Required: flat surface like tables, wall space to post

Activity Description:

1. Give each person a puzzle piece (laminated).
2. Find the people who have other puzzle pieces for that cartoon.
3. They put puzzle pieces together and glue on chart paper.
4. As a group they create a caption about how they feel today, their reaction to a situation, etc.
5. Write caption on flip chart paper, present to larger group and post.

Line-up

Primary
Junior
Intermediate
Senior

Group Size: whole class

Time Line: 3-4 minutes

Equipment Needed: students need no equipment

Space Required: entire room

Activity Description:

1. Students are to line up by hair colour, or height, or shoe size, or birthday, or address, or telephone number.
2. Students cannot speak during the activity and must communicate non-verbally.
3. Once lined up, count and divide into groups of 3 or 4 as desired.
4. Once groups are formed, give them the task of forming as many words as possible from a larger word like: distribute, moderation, consideration, motivate.
5. See how many they can make and what they are.

40

House of Cards

Group Size: class sizes (52 or less)

Time Line: 5 minutes

Equipment Needed: deck of cards

Space Required: classroom

Activity Description:

1. Student comes in door and gets card.
2. Quiet group down.
3. Divide by colours - 2 groups.
4. Divide by suits - 4 groups.
5. Divide by even numbers - 2 groups.
6. Divide by odd numbers - 2 groups.
7. Divide by card number (i.e. Aces) - groups of 4.

Primary
Junior
Intermediate
Senior

"Sorting" into Groups

Group Size: whole class

Time Line: short

Equipment Needed: none

Space Required: classroom

Activity Description:

1. To collect students into groups quickly, call on "anyone with shoelaces", "blond hair", or "anyone wearing jeans", etc.
2. If groups need to be smaller, refine "anyone with blue jeans and a sweater".
3. Once in groups, find as many common qualities or characteristics as possible without using the category under which they assembled.

Primary
Junior
Intermediate
Senior

41

Jigsaw #1

Primary
Junior
Intermediate
Senior

Group Size: whole class

Time Line: dependent on group size

Equipment Needed: large pieces of a single puzzle

Space Required: large enough for free movement

Activity Description:

1. Give out pieces of puzzle.
2. Each finds one person who has piece that fits.
3. Partners find another set that fits, etc.
4. Requires co-operation.
5. Can be done in silence, timed, etc.
6. Works well as a group "getting to know you" activity.
7. Try leaving pieces out and have small groups draw in the missing pieces using inference.

Alphabet Line-up

Primary
Junior
Intermediate
Senior

Group Size: whole class

Time Line: 5-10 minutes

Equipment Needed: none

Space Required: perimeter of classroom

Activity Description:

1. Children line up so first names/last names are in alphabetical order.
2. Then form random groups of any size by counting off.

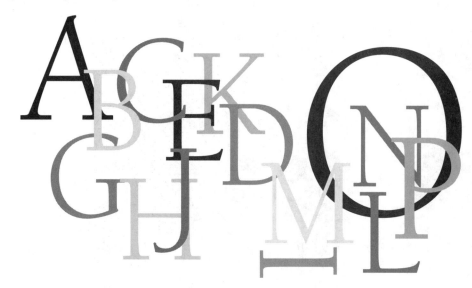

What's This Got To Do With Anything • Jim Craigen & Chris Ward
Kagan Publishing • 1 (800) 933-2667 • www.KaganOnline.com

Numbers or Head-to-Head

Group Size: whole class - work down to groups of 5/6

Time Line: no more than 5 minutes

Equipment Needed: none, physical space (move desks, chairs)

Space Required: open area, 1/2 class or so

Activity Description:

1. Know how many students are present, so that you'll be able to figure out groupings.
2. Students will arrange themselves in groups according to the number given by teacher and how the group should interact. i.e. "5 - toe to toe"
3. The leftover children move to the side of the class.
4. Continue with more examples: "4 - elbow to elbow"; then increase speed, etc.
5. Continue and when students get down to 5 or 6, rather than having a winner (or pair), you make a number based on a group they won't be able to do. i.e 5 kids left → "pinky to pinky, 7".
6. On a few occasions, students will pull in kids from the side (very creative!).
7. Students have fun doing it. You could also stop at groups of 4, 3, etc. and keep those as your cooperative group.

Birthday Game

Group Size: whole class

Time Line: as quickly as possible

Equipment Needed: nothing

Space Required: classroom/gym/outside

Activity Description:

1. Students arrange themselves in order according to their birthdates from youngest to oldest.
2. Form groups of any size.

43

Grouping By Sitcoms

Group Size: whole class

Time Line: three minutes

Equipment Needed: puzzle pieces (cards with sitcom characters' names, i.e. Cosby Show - Theo, Vanessa; Simpsons - Bart, Marg, Homer)

Space Required: entire classroom

Activity Description:

1. Each student will be given a card with a sitcom character's name on it.
2. Students are responsible to search for all the other characters from their sitcom.
3. When their group is complete, everyone should sit down.
4. This activity is a good welcoming activity or a mixer to get different students interacting.

Sing-a-long

Group Size: whole class

Time Line: 5-10 minutes

Equipment Needed: strips of paper with the beginning lines of well-known songs, i.e. Row, Row, Row Your Boat, etc.

Space Required: room to move around

Activity Description:

1. Everyone is given a piece of paper with the opening line of a common song or nursery rhyme.
2. By singing aloud, find other people who have the same song and form a group of ?

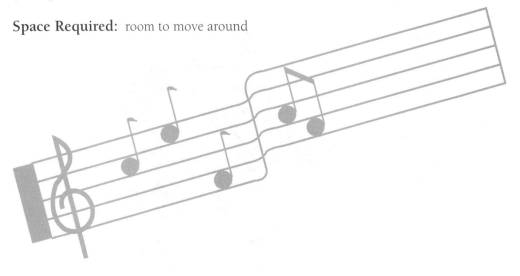

44

Animal Grouping

Group Size: whole class

Time Line: 5 minutes

Equipment Needed: strips of paper with types of animals

Space Required: classroom, gym

Activity Description:

1. Strips of paper with animal names (i.e. monkey, snake, elephant) are placed in a bag.
2. Students pick one and act out the animal they've chosen.
3. They end up in groups according to their actions or animal sounds.

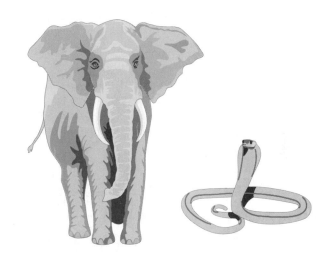

Meet Your Partner

Group Size: whole class

Time Line: 20 minutes or so

Equipment Needed: name card

Space Required: enough room to move around

Activity Description:

1. Each person is given a name card of one member of a famous couple.
2. She/he is to find her/his partner, e.g. Mickey Mouse and Minnie Mouse.
3. Next they are to find 1 other couple to form a particular category, i.e. cartoon couples, presidents/wives (political figures), actors/actresses.
4. This forms their HOME GROUP.

45

Famous Pairs

Primary
Junior
Intermediate
Senior

Group Size: whole class

Time Line: 15 minutes

Equipment Needed: 3 x 5 cards, string or tape, markers

Space Required: open area

Activity Description:

1. Number of groups needed determine types of pairs (i.e. pairs from history, royalty, comics, animation, etc.).
2. Each person has a name on his/her back.
3. Find your famous partner by asking questions (yes and no answers only).
4. Find other couples who fit your category to set up groups.

Busy Bee

Primary
Junior
Intermediate
Senior

Group Size: whole class

Time Line: 5 minutes

Equipment Needed: none

Space Required: large open space, gym, outdoors

Activity Description:

1. Students move (jog) quickly in any direction around the room.
2. Teacher calls out a number from 1 to 7, e.g. "5".
3. Students then must form a group of "5".
4. "Leftover" can be invited into centre of a group.
5. Repeat from #1 for any size of group.

46

X's and O's

Primary
Junior
Intermediate
Senior

Group Size: 9 or more, preferably multiples of 9

Time Line: 5-7 minutes

Equipment Needed: X's and O's grid - could be made out of masking tape on floor; X or O label for each person

Space Required: each grid - 6 ft. x 6 ft. (approximately), x number of grids needed

Activity Description:

1. Number off groups of 9; 5 wear X's, 4 wear O's.
2. Each group of 9 go to grid, play X's and O's.
3. With 1's starting, go in order.
4. Each winning group of 3 becomes a team.
5. Play until all become a winning combo.
6. Join another group (grid) and continue to play until all have become groups of 3.

Spell It

Primary
Junior
Intermediate
Senior

Group Size: whole class

Time Line: 10-15 minutes

Equipment Needed: pool of words on chart paper (# of letters = # of people in each group) (same number as desired # of groups, e.g. 7 words means 7 groups)

Space Required: varies depending on size of group

Activity Description:

1. Have each letter on a paper square - give 1 to each person.
2. Each person walks around, looking for another who can match letters of a word from chart.
3. The 2 then look for the 3rd, etc. until they can spell a word.
4. The group which spells a word becomes a team.

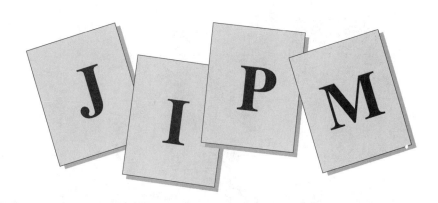

47

Jigsaw Puzzle

Primary
Junior
Intermediate
Senior

Group Size: whole class - clusters of 4-6

Time Line: 5-10 minutes

Equipment Needed: 1 picture per group, glued onto a piece of construction paper (depending on level of students, this picture can be more or less, abstract/complicated)

Space Required: regular classroom

Activity Description:

1. Use a different coloured piece of construction paper for each group you will have.
2. Cut up picture into number of pieces that match number of people you want in each group (cut up jigsaw style).
3. Mix all pieces from all puzzles in a large basket.
4. As students come in, they each take a puzzle piece at random.
5. At a signal from teacher, students must find people with missing pieces and put together the puzzle.
6. Now you have a group ready to do whatever task!

Hidden Numerals

Primary
Junior
Intermediate
Senior

Group Size: whole class (multiple of 4)

Time Line: 5-10 minutes

Equipment Needed: groups of 4 sequential numbers (4, 5, 6, 7), tape

Space Required: classroom

Activity Description:

1. Tape numerals on back of people.
2. Without talking (hand gestures only)
3. Find 3 other members of your group (e.g. 3, 4, 5, 6) (15, 16, 17, 18).

48

Shake Hands with a Friend

Group Size: will vary - two or more players per group

Time Line: 5 to 10 minutes

Equipment Needed: none

Space Required: classroom

Activity Description:

1. This game is carried out without talking.
2. This game is a quick way to introduce players to each other in a safe and non-threatening manner.
3. Count off players by ones, twos, threes, and so on, up to the number of teams required.
4. Everyone walks around the room shaking hands with each other.
5. A player whose number is "one" shakes the other player's hand once. If the number is "two", shake twice, etc.
6. One player will stop shaking while the other continues, if each player has a different number.
7. Players with identical numbers will form a group and look for other players with the same number.
8. Each group member must shake the hand of a newcomer.

What's This Got To Do With Anything • Jim Craigen & Chris Ward
Kagan Publishing • 1 (800) 933-2667 • www.KaganOnline.com

Now that you have them in groups, here's what you can do next!

Group/Class Builders

WHAT'S THIS GOT TO DO WITH ANYTHING?

Three Blind Mice

Group Size: 4 per group

Time Line: Plan and Practice - 10 minutes; Present - 5 minutes

Equipment Needed: none

Space Required: 3 metre square for each group

Activity Description:

1. Each group plans and practises actions for Three Blind Mice.
2. Each group in turn presents to the other groups as whole class sings.
3. Extend by going to classes around the school - each group to different rooms.

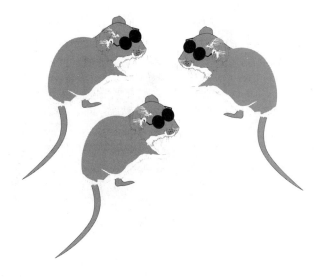

Who is Missing?

Group Size: any size

Time Line: 5-10 minutes

Equipment Needed: none

Space Required: floor space for a large circle

Activity Description:

1. Children form large circle.
2. Sit down - bend heads downward with eyes closed.
3. Teacher moves quietly around circle - gently touching 1 child on the shoulder.
4. That child quietly leaves room (stands in hallway).
5. Children then stand up - change places.
6. Then look around circle to see who is missing.
7. Ask child who puts hand up first.
8. Do this 4 or 5 times.
9. **Don't forget to call child in from hallway.**

53

What's This Got To Do With Anything • Jim Craigen & Chris Ward
Kagan Publishing • 1 (800) 933-2667 • www.KaganOnline.com

Keep It Up

Primary
Junior
Intermediate
Senior

Group Size: 17-25 (larger numbers for younger children)

Time Line: couple of minutes

Equipment Needed: parachute, or large sheet (for small group), utility ball or similar

Space Required: open floor space with adequate ceiling height or outside

Activity Description:

1. People spaced equally around outer border of parachute, moving parachute up and down as a ball moves, bounces and generally stays in motion. (Good as an introduction activity to other activities in parachute play.)

Memory Game

Primary
Junior
Intermediate
Senior

Group Size: whole group

Time Line: 1-5 minutes

Equipment Needed: tray, 12 assorted objects, scarf, pencil, paper

Space Required: table top

Activity Description:

1. 12 objects are displayed on the tray and covered with the scarf.
2. Groups gather around table, unveil the tray, and give students 30 seconds to silently observe the tray.
3. Cover tray and have each group list as many objects as they can remember.

54

Getting To Know One Another

Group Size: partners - group of 4

Time Line: approximately 10 minutes

Equipment Needed: paper, markers

Space Required: classroom

Activity Description:

1. In pairs, draw each others' hand and share 5 pieces of information about yourself filling in the fingers.
2. Introduce this new friend (5 pieces of information) to 2 others in your group of 4.

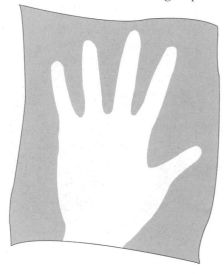

My Favourite Food

Group Size: small groups (no more than 8)

Time Line: 5 minutes

Equipment Needed: none

Space Required: enough for group to form circles

Activity Description:

1. Each child says his/her name in group and states what their favourite food is when they say their name.
2. As each person speaks, he/she has to say what was said previously and add their own name/food.
3. Continue around group until all have contributed.

55

Touching Toes

Primary
Junior
Intermediate
Senior

Group Size: 8-12

Time Line: 1-2 minutes

Equipment Needed:

Space Required: enough to come together

Activity Description:

1. Students stand in groups of 8-12 with right foot forward, all toes touching in the centre.
2. They attempt to hold each other up so they can get their left feet off the ground.
3. Ask them to count the seconds they are in position and they try to beat their record.

60 Second Math Warm-up

Primary
Junior
Intermediate
Senior

Group Size: varies

Time Line: 60 seconds

Equipment Needed: watch with second hand

Space Required: classroom

Activity Description:

1. In 15 seconds tap your feet as fast as you can. Record the number.
2. In 15 seconds snap your fingers. Record the number.
3. In 15 seconds blink your eyes. Record the number.
4. In 15 seconds clap your hands. Record the number.
5. Tally up the count and share your scores.

What's This Got To Do With Anything • Jim Craigen & Chris Ward
Kagan Publishing • 1 (800) 933-2667 • www.KaganOnline.com

Name Poster

Group Size: whole class in groups of 4 or 5

Time Line: 3-5 minutes group brainstorming and 2 minutes whole class sharing

Equipment Needed: 12" x 18" piece of construction paper per group; coloured marking pens

Space Required: floor or table

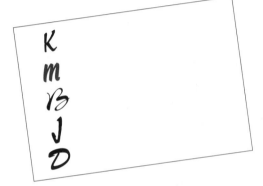

Activity Description:

1. Each group prints the first initial of every group member down the left side of the paper.
2. Within three minutes, each team is to come up with a positive phrase or word to describe every team member.
3. The phrase or word must begin with the same letter as the initial.
4. Students write down the comments on the paper.
5. They reconvene as a whole class and share their poster and the descriptions of each member.
6. Posters may be saved and used as "Group posters" for group gatherings.

Group Chant

Group Size: whole class

Time Line: 1 minute

Equipment Needed: none

Space Required: anywhere

Activity Description:

1. This method can be used to introduce a new word that you want to discuss, or as a review or to teach spelling.
2. It is based on the "cheerleader" cheer.

Leader -	Class Response
Give me an "E"	E
Give me an "N"	N
Continue . . .	
What have you got?	"Energizer"

57

"Me" Boxes

Primary
Junior
Intermediate
Senior

Group Size: whole class — 4-6 people per group

Time Line: 3 days

Equipment Needed: box to hold descriptors; items to share about oneself

Space Required: 1/4 of a classroom

Activity Description:

1. Bring in 5 items that tell about yourself.
2. This could include your hobbies, family, favourite trip, background information, etc.
3. Your items must fit into the box you choose.
4. You may decorate your box.
5. Great for all ability groups and the creative child!
6. Share with your other team members.

Draw A Critter

Primary
Junior
Intermediate
Senior

Group Size: whole class

Time Line: 30-40 minutes

Equipment Needed: paper/pencil/ crayons

Space Required: classroom

Activity Description:

1. Children are divided into groups of three to draw a critter.
2. Each child gets one sheet of paper and divides it into thirds by folding horizontally.
3. Then, each student uses the top third to draw the head of the critter adding guidelines for the next person to continue the body without having seen the head.
4. Allow ten minutes for this part of the activity.
5. The head is folded inside.
6. The second person completes body in ten minutes, then hides it for the third person to complete the lower portion in ten minutes.
7. It is then returned to the starter who then colours and names the critter.
8. All the critters are then displayed.
9. This activity can be integrated into Language Arts by doing a writing activity based on the critters.

What's This Got To Do With Anything • Jim Craigen & Chris Ward
Kagan Publishing • 1 (800) 933-2667 • www.KaganOnline.com

Middle Initial Game

Primary
Junior
Intermediate
Senior

Group Size: whole class

Time Line: 12-15 minutes

Equipment Needed: tally sheet

Space Required: classroom space to form a circle

Activity Description:

1. Students form a circle.
2. The student whose birthday is closest to January 1st, or December 31st, etc. is "it" and stands in the centre of the circle.
3. He/she points to someone in the circle; that person in turn gives his/her middle name initial.
4. The person who is "it" has 30 seconds to name as many things as possible that start with that letter.
5. The person in the centre (it) switches places with person in outside circle.
6. The new "it" chooses the next person in the circle and proceeds the same way.
7. Teacher could keep track of number of responses or another student may act as judge.

Alphabet Brainstorming

Primary
Junior
Intermediate
Senior

Group Size: whole class divided into small groups

Time Line: 10 minutes - 1/2 hour (varies with task)

Equipment Needed: paper, pencil

Space Required: classroom

Aardvark

Bull

Cat

Activity Description:

1. Divide students into small groups (4 or 5).
2. A recorder lists alphabet vertically on paper.
3. Teacher announces a topic, e.g. animals, and starts timer for 5 minutes.
4. Working in groups, students brainstorm an animal for each letter of the alphabet (may permit use of resources).
5. When 5 minutes are up, groups call out, in turn, their answer for each letter (all A's, then all B's, etc.).
6. To score a point, a group must have a "unique" animal for any given letter.

59

Human Wheel

Group Size: whole class activity

Time Line: 10-15 minutes, longer if desired

Equipment Needed: none - only students and their imagination

Space Required: gymnasium - open room; variations include various obstacles

Activity Description:

1. 1st progression - divide class into groups of 5-6 students. At first may separate boys and girls.
2. Progress to larger and mixed groups, ultimately forming a wheel with the entire class.
3. Keeping its round shape, the students must hold hands, facing into the centre of the circle, and work together to roll the "Human Wheel" along the walls of the gym.
4. Add safe and soft obstacles against the wall that the wheels must roll over.

Alphabet Describers

Group Size: groups of 3 or 4

Time Line: 10 minutes

Equipment Needed: chart paper/ markers

Space Required: classroom, working area (round table) for each group

Activity Description:

1. In groups of 3 or 4, (home group) members are to think of words which describe them, or words which they have in common - which begin with the same letter.

i.e: A - amiable, artistic, active, Ajax or
   C - cook, curious, clothes, cat lovers

Group member #1 - collect materials and timer
Group member #2 - draws the letter and writes words on it
Group member #3 - acts as the checker

Social Goal - equal participation and to encourage others

What's This Got To Do With Anything • Jim Craigen & Chris Ward
Kagan Publishing • 1 (800) 933-2667 • www.KaganOnline.com

Traffic Jam

Group Size: 2-4 or class broken into partners

Time Line: 10 minutes

Equipment Needed: paper and markers

Space Required: desk and chairs

Activity Description:

1. Work with a partner to create a vehicle for the future.
2. Your goal is to try to solve one or more of the following problems: traffic jams, fuel shortage or smog.
3. Make a drawing of the vehicle and work together to write a short description.
4. Remember to include your solutions.
5. Share your vehicle with other members of the group.

Primary
Junior
Intermediate
Senior

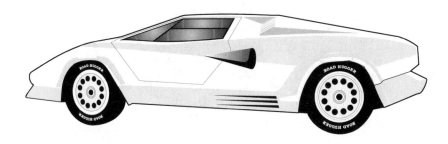

Straw Structure

Group Size: whole class

Time Line: 10-15 minutes

Equipment Needed: boxes of straws, rolls of masking tape

Space Required: classroom

Activity Description:

1. Put students in groups.
2. Give each group a box of straws and a roll of tape.
3. Tell each group to make the highest free standing structure it can by working together.
4. Give starting time and all stop when time is up.
5. Measure finished structure.

Primary
Junior
Intermediate
Senior

61

Newspaper Mix-up

Group Size: small groups (2-3, 4-5)

Time Line: 5 minutes

Equipment Needed: cut up newspaper

Space Required: small area - desks, rugs

Activity Description:

1. Have newspaper cut up into weird shapes (small/large depending on grades).
2. Without talking, the group has to work together to put the paper back together.

Creating a Monster Character

Group Size: whole class (groups of 3 or 4)

Time Line: 10 minutes

Equipment Needed: 1 coloured marker for each group member, paper for draft and final copy

Space Required: table or desk or floor

Activity Description:

1. The group is to create a monster figure (theme - "The Unknown" or "Hallowe'en").
2. Members of the group will collaborate and decide on the features.
3. If a part of the monster is to be green, only that person with the green marker can add to the monster's features.
4. The same goes for the other colours, i.e. the person with the red marker adds the red features.
5. The group will decide on a name for the monster.

62

De´deck´tive

Primary
Junior
Intermediate
Senior

Group Size: any

Time Line: 5 minutes

Equipment Needed: standard deck of
  playing cards

Space Required: classroom

Activity Description:

1. Separate and publicize the appropriate
   number of cards from the deck.
2. Each student is dealt a card which s/he
   places face out on his/her forehead
   without looking at it.
3. By looking at all other cards each
   student must deduce the suit of his/her
   card and/or deduce the denomination of
   his/her card.
   or
   Without talking, students must group
   according to suit or according to
   denomination.
   or
   Arrange themselves in denominational
   order within groups according to suit.

Where Do We Belong?

Primary
Junior
Intermediate
Senior

Group Size: any size

Time Line: varies

Equipment Needed: Post-its

Space Required: space for group line-
  ups

Activity Description:

1. Teacher writes the letters of the alphabet
   (or numbers or letters of a word or a
   number sentence) singly on post-it
   notes.
2. The post-its are then placed on students'
   foreheads. (N.B. The children do not
   know their letter or number.)
3. The group must organize itself in alphabetical or numerical order without
   speaking.

63

Appreciation

Primary
Junior
Intermediate
Senior

Group Size: regular class size divided into small groups

Time Line: 10-15 minutes

Equipment Needed: envelopes (for name strips) - one for each member; 5 copies of names of whole group cut in strips, pouch/pocket with each members' name

Space Required: classroom

Activity Description:

1. Each envelope has 5 random strips of paper with names and a blank strip.
2. Envelopes are handed out to each member.
3. Write a positive comment about the person whose name appears on the strip. Blank strip may be used as an additional positive comment if needed.
4. Positive comments are then placed into different members' pouches.

Name the Parts

Primary
Junior
Intermediate
Senior

Group Size: doesn't matter

Time Line: 2-5 minutes

Equipment Needed: paper, pencil

Space Required: classroom

Activity Description:

1. In your group, make a list of 10 body parts that only have 3 letters, e.g. lip, leg, arm.

Hint:
5 are above the neck and 5 are below.

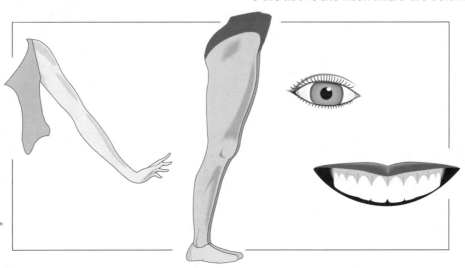

What's This Got To Do With Anything • Jim Craigen & Chris Ward
Kagan Publishing • 1 (800) 933-2667 • www.KaganOnline.com

Complete the Sequence

Group Size: class divided into groups of 2, 3 or 4

Time Line: 5-10 minutes

Equipment Needed: overhead projector or blackboard, paper and pencil

Space Required: regular classroom

Activity Description:

Have each group complete the following sequences:

1. M, V, E, M,___, ___, ___, ___, ___.
2. A, B, C, D,___, ___, ___...
3. A, D, G, J,___, ___, ___...
4. O, T, T, F, F, ___, ___, ___...
5. M, T, W, ___, ___, ___, ___
6. J, F, M, A, M, ___, ___, ___, ___, ___, ___, ___

Answer Key:

1. Planets in Solar System
2. Alphabet
3. Skip 2 letters of alphabet
4. First letters of the number words
5. Days of week
6. Months of year

It's Your Deal

Group Size: groups of 3 or 4

Time Line: 5-10 minutes

Equipment Needed: decks of cards - enough decks to supply one deck to a group of 3 or 4 students

Space Required: group gathers around a desk or in a circle on the floor

Activity Description:

1. For groups of 3 or 4.
2. One person is first dealer.
3. Teacher or class decides what will be done with the cards mathematically as they are dealt (e.g. deal 2 cards and multiply them together).
4. First person in group to shout the correct answer wins those cards.
5. Deal and play for 1 minute.
6. Gather in cards and pass the deal to person on dealer's left.
7. Change dealer and operation until each person has dealt.
8. This is an easy, quick, fun way to drill math skills.

65

Dart Math

Primary
Junior
Intermediate
Senior

Group Size: whole class

Time Line: 4-5 minutes

Equipment Needed: velcro dart board or bean bags with target on floor, pencil and paper

Space Required: classroom

Activity Description:

1. One student throws the darts.
2. It is decided ahead of time the operations, e.g. 1st dart × 2nd dart + the 3rd.
3. An official (calculator in hand) is the answer person.
4. Each group answers the question (limited time).
5. Right answer is awarded so many points.
6. Each team keeps points.
7. End of a cycle points are posted and an award is given.

Word Palindromes

Primary
Junior
Intermediate
Senior

Group Size: any

Time Line: 15 minutes

Equipment Needed: paper, pen

Space Required: any

MOM
MADAM
DAD
POP

Activity Description:

1. Teacher gives a few palindromes (words that are the same backward and forward), i.e. Nan, Madam.
2. Get kids to identify what's happening with the words, and introduce the term 'palindrome'.
3. Then have groups generate lists of palindromes.

Hint:
If they're really struggling, suggest starting with names.

What's This Got To Do With Anything • Jim Craigen & Chris Ward
Kagan Publishing • 1 (800) 933-2667 • www.KaganOnline.com

Alphabet Story

Group Size: whole class

Time Line: 5 minutes or keep going and start over

Equipment Needed: imagination

Space Required: class

Activity Description:

1. One student will start a sentence beginning with a word that starts with letter "a".
2. The next player will add a sentence with a word that starts with b, then c, d, etc.
3. It must make sense to form a story.

Primary
Junior
Intermediate
Senior

Co-operative Story

Group Size: group of 5 members

Time Line: 5-10 minutes

Equipment Needed: instruction sheet, pen

Space Required: classroom

Activity Description:

1. Each member is assigned responsibility for writing one part of a story - When? Where? Who? What happened? What were the consequences (ending)? to form a story line.
2. When assembled, the story could be collectively read orally. (This could also incorporate "the 5 W's" of a good news story.)

Primary
Junior
Intermediate
Senior

67

Express Yourself

Primary
Junior
Intermediate
Senior

Group Size: whole class

Time Line: ongoing

Equipment Needed: blackboard and chalk

Space Required: a designated piece of board "P.L.O.'d"

Activity Description:

1. The board becomes an access for anyone who has graffiti to write (there are, of course, restrictions but these are easier to apply than you might imagine).
2. Start off with just labelling the board one morning "Graffiti".
3. Then adding in a different script and colour, i.e. "I really ... and then add "I really like ANY Italian food".
4. I don't comment on what's added but it gets super as time goes on - you start looking for the add-ons!

Who Am I?

Primary
Junior
Intermediate
Senior

Group Size: whole class

Time Line: 40 minutes or less

Equipment Needed: paper, pencil

Space Required: classroom

Activity Description:

1. Each student writes a characterization of him/her self, describe self or write interests.
2. Do not write any definite descriptions to give yourself away.
3. Hand in.
4. Teacher or other student reads description.
5. Others try to guess.

What's This Got To Do With Anything • Jim Craigen & Chris Ward
Kagan Publishing • 1 (800) 933-2667 • www.KaganOnline.com

"Build A Story" Tableaux

Group Size: whole class

Time Line: 20-30 minutes

Equipment Needed: none

Space Required: anywhere the class can sit in a circle

Activity Description:

1. Have the class sit in a circle.
2. Choose 1 student to go to the centre and "freeze" into an action.
3. Tap another student on the head and have them add to the tableaux.
4. Continue until there are 8 or 9 students creating the tableaux.
5. Choose students from the circle to "tell" the story as they see it.
6. Repeat until the fun ends.

Guess The Fib

Group Size: groups of 3-4

Time Line: 5-10 minutes

Equipment Needed: none

Space Required: classroom

Activity Description:

1. Each person in the group has a turn to make three statements about himself/herself.
2. Two must be true, and one a plausible fib.
3. Others in the group try to reach consensus on which statement is the fib.

What's This Got To Do With Anything • Jim Craigen & Chris Ward
Kagan Publishing • 1 (800) 933-2667 • www.KaganOnline.com

69

Nothing To Sneeze At

Primary
Junior
Intermediate
Senior

Group Size: class divided into groups of 3-4

Time Line: 8 minutes

Equipment Needed: paper, pencils

Space Required: seating area for group, flat writing surface

Activity Description:

1. Group considers the impact on society of the following headline "Cure found for Common Cold".
2. Group records ideas as they are generated.
3. a) Group reaches a consensus - Good News or Bad News. Why?
   b) Group circles the most creative/ weird/silly idea.
4. Share with whole class.

Building Squares

Primary
Junior
Intermediate
Senior

Group Size: whole class in groups of 4

Time Line: 20-25 minutes

Equipment Needed: sets of envelopes labelled A, B, C, D, with puzzle pieces for 4 different squares in each

Space Required: classroom

Activity Description:

1. Each person in group receives envelope that has pieces of all the different squares. Initially you do not have the correct pieces to complete your square.
2. Goal is to make equal squares out of puzzle pieces.
3. Rules: no talking.
4. The only way you may get a puzzle piece from someone is if they freely give it to you.

I Am Special Because...

Group Size: whole class

Time Line: 20 minutes

Equipment Needed: "I Am Special Because..." booklets for each student made from construction paper and loose leaf paper and pens or pencils to write with

Space Required: classroom, desks or tables to write on. Allow students to circulate as they pass their booklets around

Activity Description:

1. Students pass their booklets around to each classmate to write in one reason or statement why they think that student is special.
2. POSITIVE statements only. This must be emphasized from the start.
3. The exercise could be introduced with the story "Love and the Cabbie". (See next page.)
4. Students may have the option of signing their name along with their comments.
5. Students then get to keep their own booklet after they are filled in.
6. They are to be kept to themselves and not meant to be shared with anyone else unless they want to.
7. I encourage them to take them home and share with their parents.

Primary
Junior
Intermediate
Senior

5 Minute Mystery

Group Size: groups of 4

Time Line: 7 minutes

Equipment Needed: book - 5 Minute Mysteries by Ken Sobol

Space Required: classroom

Activity Description:

1. A person reads the mystery.
2. A person records.
3. A person encourages.
4. A person probes.
5. The group comes up with ideas to solve the mystery.

Primary
Junior
Intermediate
Senior

71

Love and the Cabbie

Primary
Junior
Intermediate
Senior

I was in New York the other day and rode with a friend in a taxi. When we got out my friend said to the driver, "Thank you for the ride. You did a superb job of driving."

The taxi driver was stunned for a second. Then he said:

"Are you a wise guy or something?"

"No, my dear man, and I'm not putting you on. I admire the way you keep cool in heavy traffic."

"Yeh," the driver said and drove off.

"What was that all about?" I asked.

"I am trying to bring love back to New York," he said. "I believe it's the only thing that can save the city."

"How can one man save New York?"

"It's not one man. I believe I have made the taxi driver's day. Suppose he has twenty fares. He's going to be nice to those twenty fares because someone was nice to him. Those fares in turn will be kinder to their employees or shopkeepers or waiters or even their own families. Eventually the goodwill could spread to at least 1,000 people. Now that isn't bad, is it?"

"But you're depending on that taxi driver to pass your goodwill to others."

"I'm not depending on it," my friend said. "I'm aware that the system isn't foolproof so I might deal with 10 different people today. If, out of 10, I can make three happy, then eventually I can indirectly influence the attitudes of 3,000 more."

"It sounds good on paper," I admitted, "but I'm not sure it works in practice."

"Nothing is lost if it doesn't. It didn't take any of my time to tell that man he was doing a good job. He neither received a larger tip nor a smaller tip. If it fell on deaf ears, so what? Tomorrow there will be another taxi driver whom I can try to make happy."

"You're some kind of a nut," I said.

"That shows you how cynical you have become. I have made a study of this. The thing that seems to be lacking, besides money of course, for our postal employees, is that no one tells people who work for the post office what a good job they're doing."

"But they're not doing a good job."

"They're not doing a good job because they feel no one cares if they do or not. Why shouldn't someone say a kind word to them?"

We were walking past a structure in the process of being built and passed five workmen eating their lunch. My friend stopped. "That's a magnificent job you men have done. It must be difficult and dangerous work."

The five men eyed my friend suspiciously.

"When will it be finished?"

"June," a man grunted.

"Ah. That really is impressive. You must all be very proud."

We walked away. I said to him, "I haven't seen anyone like you since `The Man from La Mancha.'"

"When those men digest my words, they will feel better for it. Somehow the city will benefit from their happiness."

"But you can't do this all alone!" I protested. "You're just one man."

"The most important thing is not to get discouraged. Making people in the city become kind again is not an easy job, but if I can enlist other people in my campaign..."

"You just winked at a very plain looking woman," I said.

"Yes, I know," he replied. "And if she's a schoolteacher, her class will be in for a fantastic day."

Art Buchwald

(From *Looking Out, Looking In*, Addley & Towne. Holt, Rinehart & Winston)

What's This Got To Do With Anything • Jim Craigen & Chris Ward
Kagan Publishing • 1 (800) 933-2667 • www.KaganOnline.com

Winning the Big One

Primary
Junior
Intermediate
Senior

Group Size: whole class - groups of 3 or 4

Time Line: 10 minutes

Equipment Needed: pen and paper

Space Required: classroom

Activity Description:

1. In your home groups, come up with 7 or 8 ways to spend your money if you won the lottery - $1,000,000.00
2. Rank them from first to last.
3. The group must be in agreement with the ranking.

These are the national statistics of how Canadian millionaires have spent their winnings:

93%	put money in the bank
71%	share winnings with others who were not co-owners of lottery ticket
56%	bought a car
51%	donated to charity
44%	took a vacation or travelled
37%	paid off mortgage
29%	bought a house
27%	paid off education for self
7%	changed lifestyle
2%	bought a boat

73

What's This Got To Do With Anything • Jim Craigen & Chris Ward
Kagan Publishing • 1 (800) 933-2667 • www.KaganOnline.com

Information Sharing

Group Size: whole class

Time Line: varied

Equipment Needed: various audio visual equipment (student's choice, or what's available)

Space Required: classroom

Activity Description:

1. Students receive handout with instructions for talk to be given.
2. Each student is to prepare a 1 minute presentation giving a piece of information about himself/herself - a hobby, a memory, a special activity he/she took part in.
3. Students could make use of an audio/visual component - slides, pictures, collage, video segment, etc.
4. Presentations are done early in semester. (Not too early - trust-building first.)
5. Great for class building.

Famous People

Group Size: small groups

Time Line: 5 minutes maximum

Equipment Needed: pen/paper - 1 per group

Space Required: at a table

Activity Description:

1. Use this activity to get the groups working and thinking together.
2. Each group brainstorms 3 famous people.
3. They then choose one of those people to represent their group, ie. "The Atwood's".
4. Then they create a banner that depicts the name and that person's contribution to history.

What's This Got To Do With Anything • Jim Craigen & Chris Ward
Kagan Publishing • 1 (800) 933-2667 • www.KaganOnline.com

Looking For Similar Interests

Group Size: groups of 4

Time Line: 5 minutes

Equipment Needed: large sheets and markers

Space Required: normal classroom

Activity Description:

1. Groups are asked to list their two top recording artists with one reason for each.
2. A tally is taken for class and percentages are made up for the individual artists.
3. They could get together in another group by artists for a quick get together.

Primary
Junior
Intermediate
Senior

Creating Our Identity

Group Size: class divided into groups of 3 or 4

Time Line: 40 minutes

Equipment Needed: chart paper, almanacs, markers

Space Required: classroom

Activity Description:

1. In the introduction, incorporate 'Multicultural' awareness of flags of the world, province emblems, etc.
2. As part of the 'no criticism' brainstorming process, the students will generate a set 'selection criteria' for choosing the 'winning entry'.
3. Brainstorm as a home-based group of 3 or 4 to generate a list of items that your group could use to select an item from to represent who they are (e.g. Teddy Bear Mascot, Flag, Logo).

Primary
Junior
Intermediate
Senior

75

Famous Numbers

Primary
Junior
Intermediate
Senior

Group Size: groups of 3-4

Time Line: 15 minutes

Equipment Needed: questionnaire

Space Required: not a real concern - corner groups

Activity Description:

1. Using the number coded messages, teams decipher common units of measure and commonly used numerical phrases.

Questions

1. 26 = L. of A.
2. 7 = W. of the W.
3. 1001 = A. N.
4. 12 = S. of the Z.
5. 54 = C. in a D. (incl. the J's)
6. 9 = P. in the S. S.
7. 88 = P. K.
8. 18 = H. on a G. C.
9. 90 = D. in a R. A.
10. 3 = B. M. (S. H. T. R.)
11. 24 = H. in a D.
12. 1 = W. on a U.
13. 57 = H. V.
14. 1000 = W. that a P. is W.
15. 29 = D. in F. in a L. Y.

16. 40 = D. and N. of the G. F.
17. 100 = CM. in a M.
18. 212 = B. P. of W. (in F.)
19. 360 = D. in a C.
20. 52 = W. in the Y.
21. 4 = Q. in a D.
22. 13 = G. in S. in O.
23. 454 = G. in a P.
24. 1 = H. in O. in G.
25. 2001 = S. O.
26. 13 = B. L.
27. 365 = D. in the Y.
28. 4 = D. on a S.
29. 13 = B's. D.
30. 7 = D. of the W.

Answers

1. Letters of the Alphabet
2. Wonders of the World
3. Arabian Nights
4. Signs of the Zodiac
5. Cards in a Deck (including the Jokers)
6. Planets in the Solar System
7. Piano Keys
8. Holes on the Golf Course
9. Degrees in a Right Angle
10. Blind Mice (See How They Run)
11. Hours in a Day
12. Wheel on a Unicycle
13. Heinz Varieties
14. Words that a Picture is worth
15. Days in February in a Leap Year

16. Days and Nights of the Great Flood
17. Centimetres in a Metre
18. Boiling Point of Water (in Fahrenheit)
19. Degrees in a Circle
20. Weeks in a Year
21. Quarters in a Dollar
22. Grades in School in Ontario
23. Grams in a Pound
24. Hole in One in Golf
25. Space Odyssey
26. Bad Luck
27. Days in the Year
28. Doors on a Sedan
29. Baker's Dozen
30. Days of the Week

76

It's The Cat's Meow

Primary
Junior
Intermediate
Senior

Group Size: whole class divided into groups of 3-4

Time Line: 10-15 minutes maximum

Equipment Needed: assignment, pen

Space Required: classroom

Activity Description:

1. Students work in groups to answer the questions.
2. All of the answers must contain the initial syllable "cat".
3. The vocabulary involved is fairly difficult to identify.

Examples:

1. What cat plays baseball?   catcher
2. What cat is a subterranean country?   catacomb
3. What cat is a sailboat?   catamaran
4. What cat is a tree?   catalpa (pussywillow)
5. What cat can be used to hunt with?   catapult
6. What cat is a waterfall?   cataract
7. What cat is a calamity?   catastrophe
8. What cat is found in church?   catechism
9. What cat is a class of things?   category
10. What cat is a fuzzy creature?   caterpillar
11. What cat is aromatic?   catnip
12. What cat is a condiment?   catsup
13. What cat is a cowboy's friend?   cattle
14. What cat is at home in the swamp?   cattail

77

Imaginative Vocabulary Interpretation

Primary
Junior
Intermediate
Senior

Group Size: full class, groups of 3 or 4

Time Line: 2-3 classes

Equipment Needed: short story text, paper, markers, drama props

Space Required: entire room or more

Activity Description:

1. Groups analyze a story/passage for significant/poetic words.
2. Write a poem using only the words from the text.
3. Group will dramatize their poem and present their skit to the class using mime, dialogue, costuming, props, etc.

Word Magic

Primary
Junior
Intermediate
Senior

Group Size: groups of 2, 3, 4

Time Line: 1-10 minutes

Equipment Needed: paper, pencils

Space Required: classroom

Activity Description:

1. Depending on your subject, you choose a title, e.g. Lake Vista Public School, Remembrance Day Ceremony, etc.
2. The students in their groups come up with as many words contained in the letters of this title as possible within a CERTAIN TIME.
3. Kids really love this, especially if there is a timer on.

What's This Got To Do With Anything • Jim Craigen & Chris Ward
Kagan Publishing • 1 (800) 933-2667 • www.KaganOnline.com

Crayola

Group Size: variable - groupings of 2-4, needs at least two groups

Time Line: variable

Equipment Needed: paper, pencil

Space Required: classroom

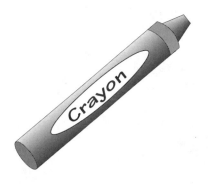

Activity Description:

1. Groupings of 2 to 4 - each with colour name.
2. In given time think of things that are same colour as you.

or

Using the same letters as the name your colour begins with, think of things that fly, things that can be driven, things in the water, things on the land, things in the air.

or

Think of noun, verb beginning with your colour letter.

3. This list may go as far as you like.
4. May stop after one task and tally colour group against colour group or have a running tally and compare.
5. Make into sentences and share.

Shout Out A Synonym

Group Size: groups of 3 or 4

Time Line: 2 or 3 minutes

Equipment Needed: paper, pencil

Space Required: a room

Activity Description:

Roles:
a) Speaker   b) Recorder
c) Encourager   d) Time Keeper

1. Teacher gives speaker a list of 10 words (e.g. bad, good, etc.).
2. Speaker shouts out word, rest list as many synonyms as possible in 30 seconds.
3. Rotate roles and continue until all have had a turn.

79

Songsters

Primary
Junior
Intermediate
Senior

Group Size: groups of 4

Time Line: 30-40 minutes

Equipment Needed: examples of familiar songs on charts

Space Required: regular groupings - perhaps necessary to move to hall, etc. as this could be noisier than usual

Activity Description:

1. Pick a familiar tune that everyone in your group knows, i.e. Row Row Row Your Boat.
2. Brainstorm ideas about the people in your group - could be commonalities, etc.
3. Develop your own words to the song that reflect a characteristic of each member of the team.
4. Present to whole classroom.

Adjective Wardrobe

Primary
Junior
Intermediate
Senior

Group Size: class group or small group within large group

Time Line: 15 minutes

Equipment Needed: markers, paper, scissors

Space Required: desk, tables, floor

Activity Description:

1. Piece of paper torn into 8 pieces by student - each student has 8 pieces of paper.
2. Students should be as honest as possible and write 8 descriptive adjectives to describe themselves.
3. They now have a wardrobe of descriptive words that can be tried on, worn or discarded.
4. Consider one word at a time. Like it? Keep it? Expand it? Discard it?
5. Give up each quality - do you feel naked? How are you changed?
6. Fantasize about kind of person he/she would be with one, two, three or all qualities removed.
7. Reclaim qualities one at a time. How do you feel now?
8. End of exercise ask each student to record 2 things learned about himself/herself.
9. Share "I learned ..." statements.

This Is For The Birds

Primary
Junior
Intermediate
Senior

Group Size: whole class

Time Line: 10-15 minutes

Equipment Needed: paper, pen/
pencil/markers, chart paper

Space Required: classroom

Activity Description:

1. In your groups, name as many birds as
   you can by:
   a) alphabet
   b) colour
   c) country
   d) continent

Variation - animals, foods, etc.

Monster Races

Primary
Junior
Intermediate
Senior

Group Size: groups of 3, 4 or 5

Time Line: 5 minutes

Equipment Needed: none

Space Required: open space - gym or
field

Activity Description:

1. Task - To get your group across the finish line (5 → 10 m away) after meeting
   the criteria.
2. Criteria - You must make a "MONSTER"
   using 8 legs and 2 arms. All members of
   the group must be joined together and
   the monster must cross the finish line
   without falling apart.
3. Extra Challenges - Repeat but alter
   criteria. E.g. Add 1 arm, 1 head, etc.

   Key - Try to use total # legs possible
   and subtract 2. E.g. 4 people, therefore
   8 legs -2 = 6 legs can be used.

81

The Web

Primary
Junior
Intermediate
Senior

Group Size: 10-15

Time Line: 10-15 minutes

Equipment Needed: ball of wool

Space Required: room to make a circle

Activity Description:

1. The teacher starts and tells something about himself/herself.
2. She/he throws the ball of wool (holding onto the end of the yarn) across to a student.
3. The student says something personal about himself/herself.
4. Then the student throws the ball to another student but makes sure that he/she still hangs onto the wool.
5. Continue until every student is connected thus making a web.

Variation:
retrace your tosses.

Sentence Structure

Primary
Junior
Intermediate
Senior

Group Size: 3 students in each group

Time Line: 5 minutes

Equipment Needed: sentence cut into either words or phrases

Space Required: classroom

Activity Description:

1. Cut sentence into words or phrases.
2. Co-operatively the group puts them together.
3. Try to use sentences that could be put together in various ways.
4. Teacher acts as a checker.
5. Could teach "grammar skills" depending on the needs of the students.

be use that try could to put sentences various together ways in

Object of Value

Primary
Junior
Intermediate
Senior

Group Size: any size

Time Line: will vary

Equipment Needed: none

Space Required: any

Activity Description:

1. Each person takes a piece of personal property of value to himself/herself, and after telling the importance, exchanges it.
2. He/she can then exchange again as often as wanted, or keep the first object received for any set time (less than one day).
3. With each exchange the story of the object's value is retold.

Magic Eleven

Primary
Junior
Intermediate
Senior

Group Size: 3 or 4

Time Line: 2-3 minutes

Equipment Needed: none

Space Required: any space

Activity Description:

1. Group the children into 3's or 4's.
2. Children stand and put one hand behind back.
3. The children form a fist with the other hand and move their fist to the count 1, 2, 3. On 3, the children must show a number of fingers.
4. The game proceeds until the group attains the number eleven when the fingers are added together.
5. This is to be done silently.
6. Groups sit down when they attain the number eleven.

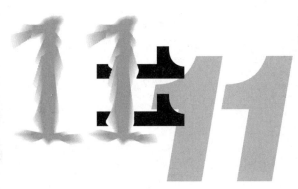

83

Identification

Group Size: whole class

Time Line: 5-10 minutes

Equipment Needed: teacher provides identification chart, pen/pencil

Space Required: minimal

Activity Description:

1. Pick an unknown student and get a detailed description of him/her for you only.
2. Have student visit your class and walk up to you and deliver a piece of paper and then he/she leaves.
3. Approximately ten minutes later hand out an identification chart. Tell students a crime has been committed. They are the witnesses. They must fill out an identification chart. (i.e. height, weight, clothing, etc.)
4. In pairs of two or small groups, collaboratively complete chart. Have students call out their answers - perhaps they could write their choices on a piece of paper.
5. Give them about 5 minutes to get the students to arrive at a consensus.
6. Then have unknown student revisit class so they can see just how good they would be as a witness.

Name That Tune

Group Size: groups of 3-4

Time Line: 3-4 minutes maximum

Equipment Needed: tape recorder, pre-taped excerpts

Space Required: classroom

Activity Description:

1. Students stand up within home groups.
2. A tape excerpt is played of maximum 3-5 *small* snippets of songs.
3. Answers are given by students.
4. Teacher can either keep a running total of correct answers so groups that better their number of correct answers receive rewards or just do it as a fun break.

What's This Got To Do With Anything • Jim Craigen & Chris Ward
Kagan Publishing • 1 (800) 933-2667 • www.KaganOnline.com

Name the Product

Group Size: class divided into small groups

Time Line: 5 minutes

Equipment Needed: 1 overhead with slogans listed

Space Required: classroom

Activity Description:

Tell the students to name the product for the slogan given:

Primary
Junior
Intermediate
Senior

1. Don't leave home without it → American Express
2. Quality is Job 1 → Ford
3. It's the real thing → Coke
4. Just do it → Nike
5. Food, Folks and Fun → McDonald's
6. A _____ moment → Kodak
7. The Un cola → 7-up
8. _____ tastes good like a cigarette should → Winston
9. The choice of a new generation → Pepsi
10. It takes a lickin' and keeps on tickin' → Timex
11. Goods satisfactory or money refunded → Eaton's

Machine

Group Size: groups of 4-10

Time Line: 10 minutes

Equipment Needed: none

Space Required: classroom

Activity Description:

1. Each person becomes a working part of a machine.
2. The group must co-ordinate so that each person is an integral part.
3. Perform for the rest of the class.

Primary
Junior
Intermediate
Senior

85

Logic Puzzles

Primary
Junior
Intermediate
Senior

Group Size: small groups

Time Line: seconds

Equipment Needed: none

Space Required: none

Activity Description:

1. Have students work in groups to solve logic puzzles. Some examples are:

Why are 1977 dollar bills worth more than 1976 dollar bills?
- (1977 dollar cost $1977 and 1976 dollar bills cost $1976)

How can a match burn under water?
- (Hold the burning match under a glass of water)

Car A leaves Toronto at 8:45 a.m. driving at a speed of 40 km/h. Car B leaves Montreal at 10:16 a.m. driving at a speed of 37 km/h. Which car is closer to Montreal when they meet?
- (When they meet, they will be the same distance from Montreal)

Students could work in groups to create their own logic puzzles.

Take A Personal Object

Primary
Junior
Intermediate
Senior

Group Size: any size depending on "time limit"

Time Line: 10-15 minutes

Equipment Needed: a personal object, i.e. jewellery, watch, shoe, comb, etc.

Space Required: depends on size of the group

Activity Description:

1. All participants take off a personal article privately.
2. As a group (in a circle), all articles dropped into a bag.
3. First person pulls out an article, and as a group, everyone guesses who it belongs to.

What's This Got To Do With Anything • Jim Craigen & Chris Ward
Kagan Publishing • 1 (800) 933-2667 • www.KaganOnline.com

Where Do I Fit In?

Group Size: whole class

Time Line: 30 minutes

Equipment Needed: bristol board(s) cut into larger jigsaw pieces - 1 for each child and teacher, markers

Space Required: activity done at desk - finished product on bulletin board

Activity Description:

1. Put title: Where Do I Fit In? on top of bulletin board.
2. Give each student a large puzzle piece (be sure to mark the top of the puzzle with a dot (or other symbol).
3. Each student designs the puzzle piece (name, picture of favourite sport, food, etc.).
4. When finished, try to find other pieces that fit together.
5. When completed, there will be one large puzzle on board.

Coat of Arms

Group Size: whole class

Time Line: 30 minutes to 1 hour

Equipment Needed: photocopy of Coat of Arms - or they may draw their own, pencil, paper

Space Required: classroom → students work in partners or small groups of 3-4

Activity Description:

1. Each student makes his/her own Coat of Arms.
2. In quadrant 1, draw your favourite pastime.
3. In quadrant 2, draw your favourite food.
4. In quadrant 3, draw your favourite sport.
5. In quadrant 4, draw what you aspire to be.
6. Once the student finished the Coat of Arms, he or she goes to his/her partner.
7. They introduce themselves.
8. Then one partner must introduce the other to the class.

Variation:
A group creates its own Coat of Arms, with each member taking a quadrant. Group logo could go in the middle.

87

Mind Blasters

Group Size: whole class

Time Line: 5 minutes

Equipment Needed: blackboard, chalk

Space Required: classroom

Activity Description:

1. Design a series of mind blasters and have group of students decipher them. Some examples are shown here.

Mind ——— Matter	→ Mind over matter
BLOOD ——— *WATER*	→ Blood is thicker than water.
Bridge ——— Water	→ Water under the bridge.
Wear ——— Long	→ long underwear

I.A.L.A.C. (I Am Lovable And Capable)

Group Size: whole class

Time Line: beginning of year or any time to reverse negativism

Equipment Needed: I.A.L.A.C. sign for teacher/storyteller - and for each student if you wish them to similarly participate

Space Required: regular class arrangement will do

Activity Description:

1. Teacher tells a story about how a student, the age of your class, had numerous negative things said/done to him/her that diminished his/her self concept.
2. As the story is told, students may contribute to its content.
3. The storyteller rips off a piece of the I.A.L.A.C. sign off with every negative comment.
4. Afterward, process with class.

What's This Got To Do With Anything • Jim Craigen & Chris Ward
Kagan Publishing • 1 (800) 933-2667 • www.KaganOnline.com

Word Warm-Up

Group Size: groups of 3 or 4

Time Line: pairs

Equipment Needed: paper/pens - put grid on board

Space Required: desks

Activity Description:

4 x 4 grid

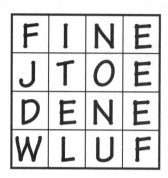

F	I	N	E
J	T	O	E
D	E	N	E
W	L	U	F

1. Find as many words as you can in a time period. Add rules as needed. (Letters must touch, etc.)

Variations:
Use list of words; highlight 5 words; write a good sentence; find a hidden, secret word.

Tiger/Hunter/Gun

Group Size: class divided into 2

Time Line: 15-20 minutes

Equipment Needed: none

Space Required: regular room

Activity Description:

1. Divide class into 2 teams.
2. Rules are 1) tiger eats hunter; 2) hunter controls gun; 3) gun shoots tiger (akin to paper, scissors, rock).
3. Groups compete against each other and decide which of the 3 choices the whole group will be.
4. Teacher says 1, 2, 3 and then each group acts either as a hunter (standing silently), a gun (by pointing finger and saying "bang") or tiger (by raising arms in air and saying "roar").
5. If both groups do the same thing, no one gets a point. If the groups do something different (and everyone in the group must do the same thing), then award a point based on the rules of the game, e.g. one group tiger, one group hunter = tiger wins.
6. Play 5 rounds to see which group can get most points.

89

Fortunately ... Unfortunately

Primary
Junior
Intermediate
Senior

Group Size: groups of 3-4

Time Line: varies (could end up publishing story for self or primary class)

Equipment Needed: large paper, markers (varies)

Space Required: classroom

Activity Description:

1. Brainstorm - good luck things/bad luck things.
2. Start story with a good luck sentence and continue:
   Fortunately I won a million dollars.
   Unfortunately I was robbed.
   Fortunately I have some clues to give to the police.
   and so on ... (length will vary)

Headbands

Primary
Junior
Intermediate
Senior

Group Size: whole class in small groups

Time Line: 3-5 minutes

Equipment Needed: construction paper strips, masking tape, marker

Space Required: open corners

Activity Description:

Assuming 4 per group.

1. One person wears a headband with something, unknown to the wearer, written on it. i.e. feeling, character, career ...
2. All other group members help the wearer guess the word on the headband by taking on specific roles.
   (a) give non-verbal clues
   (b) silent partner
   (c) speak in jargon of the topic.
3. Depending on the topic, other roles may be more appropriate.

What's This Got To Do With Anything • Jim Craigen & Chris Ward
Kagan Publishing • 1 (800) 933-2667 • www.KaganOnline.com

Untie The Knot

Group Size: divided into uneven groups of 7, 9, 11 etc.

Time Line: 10 minutes

Equipment Needed: none

Space Required: classroom (move desks out of the way)

Activity Description:

1. In a group of uneven numbered people, all except one person links right hands. Do not join hands with a person beside you.
2. Then join left hands with a different person. One person does not join up.
3. One person is left with left hand out and one person is left with right hand out.
4. Untie the knot. Don't let go.

Historical Identity

Group Size: any size group

Time Line: as long as necessary depending on how many

Equipment Needed: none

Space Required: classroom

Activity Description:

1. Teacher gives instruction: If you could have been any person in history who would it be and why?
2. Give students 30 seconds to 1 minute to think.
3. Share round-robin.
4. *Variation*: Names could be characters from books, movies, sports, etc.

91

Code

Group Size: whole class divided into groups 3-4

Time Line: 5 minutes

Equipment Needed: none

Space Required: open space class

Activity Description:

1. Have students develop a simple code, i.e. numbers for letters of the alphabet.
2. Every second or third day have an encrypted "positive" statement on the board.

3 1 7 6 4

That's Entertainment

Group Size: whole class

Time Line: 5 minutes

Equipment Needed: pen and paper

Space Required: classroom setting

Activity Description:

1. Set up the home groupings.
2. Explain to the entire class that they are to list the Top 10 North American TV Shows. (must explain that this list is for 1991 and that The Simpsons' started in 1991-92)
3. Give up to 5 minutes for group discussion (home group).
4. Uncover list on overhead step-by-step or ask for numbered member of group to read out an answer.

1991 Top 10 TV Programs (North American)

1. 60 Minutes
2. Cheers
3. America's Funniest Home Videos
4. America's Funniest People
5. Murder, She Wrote
6. Murphy Brown
7. NFL Monday Night Football
8. Roseanne
9. Designing Women
10. Unsolved Mysteries

Update with current year's information on T.V. or films etc.

What's This Got To Do With Anything • Jim Craigen & Chris Ward
Kagan Publishing • 1 (800) 933-2667 • www.KaganOnline.com

Jigsaw #2

Group Size: any size

Time Line: 3 minutes

Equipment Needed: 1 jigsaw puzzle per group (any jigsaw shape...a cut up magazine picture works well)

Space Required: 1 flat surface (tabletop) per group

Activity Description:

1. Have each group member number off.
2. Each jigsaw piece is numbered on back.
3. Member takes his/her numbered piece and group works together to form puzzle.
4. Members can offer help, suggestions, etc. but cannot take any other member's piece out of his/her hands.
5. This is especially fun and challenging when done as a silent activity - no *verbal* help or suggestions.

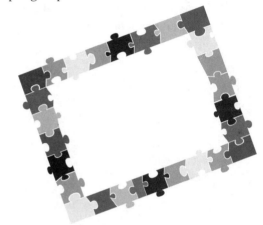

Ballbearing

Group Size: groups of 4 or 5

Time Line: 5-10 minutes

Equipment Needed: paper, pen

Space Required: classroom

Activity Description:

1. Place students in teams of 4 or 5.
2. Number each member.
3. Teams are to brainstorm as many uses for ballbearings as they can in 5 minutes.
4. Each team member is to record team responses.
5. The team that has come up with the greatest number of uses wins a prize.
6. Branch team members off into share groups. (i.e. all #1's get together, #2's etc.)
7. Have group members share ideas.

93

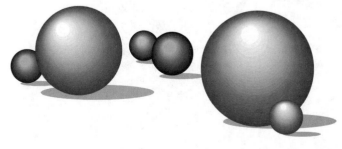

Team Cheer

Group Size: groups of 3 or 4

Time Line: 3 minutes

Equipment Needed: voices!

Space Required: gym (probably) or outside

Activity Description:

1. After having taught a specific skill and after students have spent time practising it, quickly put them in groups of 3 or 4 and have them come up with a cheer that loudly encourages the skill.
2. Have each group quickly do the cheer for the rest.
3. Then proceed on with a new skill.
4. This would promote positive interaction and encouragement.

Group Cheer

Group Size: 3-8

Time Line: 10 minutes

Equipment Needed: none

Space Required: any

Activity Description:

1. Each group must incorporate its name or identity into a cheer or song which will then be presented to the class.

What's This Got To Do With Anything • Jim Craigen & Chris Ward
Kagan Publishing • 1 (800) 933-2667 • www.KaganOnline.com

Nifty Numbers

Group Size: groups of three or pairs

Time Line: 10-30 minutes

Equipment Needed: pencil/paper

Space Required: minimal

Activity Description:

1. With your partner(s), agree on one number between 1 and 9.
2. Brainstorm for as many ideas/items as possible that include or represent that number.
3. Represent each idea on a mind map.

Cooperative Balloon Pass

Group Size: 4-8 to a group

Time Line: 5 minutes

Equipment Needed: one balloon per group, chair for each student

Space Required: area for chairs to be set up in a circle for each group

Activity Description:

1. Sit on chairs in circle.
2. Pass balloon 3 times around circle using feet.
3. Last person 3rd round sits on balloon and breaks it - Finished!

95

How Many Items In A ...?

Group Size: whole class divided into smaller groups

Time Line: 5 minutes but could be 30 minutes if you're a supply teacher and need to get organized

Equipment Needed: pen and paper

Space Required: not necessary

Activity Description:

1. Brainstorm all the items you would need to buy for a kitchen, sailboat, classroom, museum, etc.
2. Works well individually or in small groups.

Alliteration Adjectives

Group Size: whole class

Time Line: depends on size of group

Equipment Needed: none

Space Required: small circles (work it out to suit your environment)

Activity Description:

1. Each person gives an adjective beginning with the same letter starting their name. e.g. Adorable Alison
2. Next person points to and says Adorable Alison, and continues to give his/her expanded name, e.g. Nervous Norm.
3. Continue around the circle.

Joyful Jessica !

What's This Got To Do With Anything • Jim Craigen & Chris Ward
Kagan Publishing • 1 (800) 933-2667 • www.KaganOnline.com

Guess The Word

Primary
Junior
Intermediate
Senior

Group Size: groups of 3 with however many students are in the class

Time Line: 1.5 minutes (30 seconds/ student)

Equipment Needed: 3 cards per group - 5 words printed on each card, i.e. cat, stop sign, sunglasses, grasshopper, treehouse (whatever group of words you want) and should be able to be held in palm of hand so that other team members cannot read it while descriptions are given

Space Required: regular class

Activity Description:

1. Have 3 students in each group.
2. Two will describe and guess words, and the third will time.
3. One student will pick a card and begin to describe the word to the student who is guessing.
4. The describer cannot use the word being described in the description. e.g. stop sign - description: a sign with eight sides.
5. The timer should time the describer and guesser giving 30 seconds.
6. The guesser must see how many he/she can guess in 30 seconds.
7. Then the group should switch roles, i.e. timer becomes describer (with a new card), describer becomes guesser, guesser becomes timer and so on until everyone has played each role.
8. Groups should add up number of words guessed.
9. Scores can be competitive against other groups, or against their previous score.

Hoola Shuffle

Primary
Junior
Intermediate
Senior

Group Size: the bigger the better - two teams or more

Time Line: 2-3 minutes

Equipment Needed: 2 hoolahoops or more

Space Required: room to divide into two long lines

Activity Description:

1. All are to hold hands.
2. Without letting go, pass hoolahoop from end to end and back again.
3. First group finished wins.

97

Stories With Symbols

Group Size: whole class

Time Line: 20 minutes

Equipment Needed: squares of construction paper (15 cm) with a symbol drawn on each (one for each participant)

Space Required: students need to sit together

Activity Description:

1. To begin, pass the cards out to all the students face down.
2. Instruct the students not to look at them until they are told.
3. Select a student to begin a story by turning over his/her own symbol card and including that symbol or its meaning into his/her story.
4. Following this, the person to the storyteller's left takes over the story, and turns over his/her symbol ready to include that concept or symbol into the story.
5. When the story reaches the last person, he/she must end the story including their symbol.

Build A Better Bathtub

Group Size: whole class

Time Line: 20 minutes

Equipment Needed: felt markers, large sheets of paper

Space Required: classroom - group seating plan

Activity Description:

1. Establish groups.
2. Appoint a recorder.
3. Review rules of brainstorming.
4. Outline task - Instruct groups they have 5 minutes to call out and write down as many ideas on the subject "How to design a better bathtub" - enjoyment, efficiency, comfort.
5. Recorder jots notes.
6. Stop at 5 minutes. Recorders read list.
7. Discussion, reflection, appreciation.
8. Draw new tub.

98

Standing Ovation

Primary
Junior
Intermediate
Senior

Group Size: whole class

Time Line: 1-2 minutes

Equipment Needed: none

Space Required: classroom

Activity Description:

1. Whenever there is a call for recognition, i.e. someone has mastered a particular skill, someone's birthday, an improved math score, someone doing a good deed for another, etc., recognize that person by giving them a standing ovation.
2. This will need explaining initially.
3. Extremely successful for self-esteem!

Line-Up

Primary
Junior
Intermediate
Senior

Group Size: any size determined by organizer divided into 2 lines

Time Line: 5 minutes

Equipment Needed: none or chairs can be used

Space Required:
enough to form
a long line

Activity Description:

1. People line up in a line facing each other.
2. One side of the line has 30 seconds to tell the other side of the line something about themselves, etc.
3. After 30 seconds people on one side of the line shift a space and tell the person opposite them something about themselves. (This could be a problem, a celebration, etc.)

99

Happy Intros

Primary
Junior
Intermediate
Senior

Group Size: whole class

Time Line: varies

Equipment Needed: none

Space Required: classroom

Activity Description:

1. Each student, in turn, stands up and tells his/her name and one thing that makes him/her happy.
2. Next, students go into groups of three and decide on one thing that makes all of them happy.
3. They then share this with the whole class.

Pictionary

Primary
Junior
Intermediate
Senior

Group Size: groups of 3 or 4

Time Line: varies

Equipment Needed: markers and paper, list of concepts, ideas, or things to be drawn

Space Required:
classroom

Activity Description:

1. The group is divided into co-operative teams.
2. Each group is given a list of things, concepts or ideas that they must draw. E.g. All number 1's on each team must draw the same thing, all number 2's, etc.
3. Team members must guess what their team member is drawing.
4. This can be done in the form of a relay race.

What's This Got To Do With Anything • Jim Craigen & Chris Ward
Kagan Publishing • 1 (800) 933-2667 • www.KaganOnline.com

Who's Like...?

Group Size: all

Time Line: 10 minutes

Equipment Needed: paper and pencil

Space Required: classroom

Activity Description:

1. Students are given the following headings: Animal, Colour, Food, Musical Instrument and Flower. They are to think of a person in the class and categorize him/her under those headings. (Maybe they like a particular food, or look like a certain animal, etc.)
Example: bear, black, chips, tuba, dandelion.
2. The other students in the group must think of who it is.

Who Are We Describing?

Group Size: any (more than 4)

Time Line: up to you

Equipment Needed: none

Space Required: circle - space

Activity Description:

1. The people/children should know each other fairly well to participate in this activity.
2. Everyone sits in a circle.
3. One child is asked to leave the room so she/he can't hear.
4. The group chooses a person quietly and invites the one person back in.
5. The person that was out of the room now has the opportunity to ask people questions to figure out the chosen person.
6. The trick is that the person can only ask questions that compare the person to something else (not direct question), e.g., If this person were light / animal / colour what would they be?

101

Family Portraits

Primary
Junior
Intermediate
Senior

Group Size: class

Time Line: 5-10 minutes

Equipment Needed: cards to equal number of students in class

Space Required: room to mingle

Activity Description:

1. Write names of families in 4's
   4 Smiths
   4 Kellys
   4 Browns etc.
2. Hand one to each person.
3. Students mingle in central area - exchanging name cards.
4. After 1 minute, teacher calls *Family Portraits*.
5. Students must find three other members of family and arrange selves in portrait frame.
6. Exchange again/2nd grouping.
7. Exchange again — groups are those you will be working with today.

What's This Got To Do With Anything • Jim Craigen & Chris Ward
Kagan Publishing • 1 (800) 933-2667 • www.KaganOnline.com

Energizers

Sticky Popcorn

Group Size: whole class

Time Line: 5 minutes

Equipment Needed: none

Space Required: open space in middle of room

Activity Description:

1. Pupils crouch on floor as if they are a kernel of popcorn.
2. Leader tells students that the "pot" is getting hot.
3. Students pop up from floor as if bursting into fluffy popcorn.
4. As they pop, they may touch another person.
5. They then must stick and pop around together.
6. Until all pupils are stuck together in one big ball, the pupils continue popping.

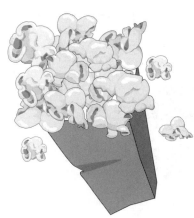

Squirrels and Trees

Group Size: 20+

Time Line: as needed for warm-up or break

Equipment Needed: none

Space Required: gym facilities or outside

Activity Description:

1. Students are numbered 1 to 3. Numbers 1 and 3 form a tree by touching fingertips.
2. The squirrels are number 2.
3. You always need to have one extra squirrel.
4. The squirrels run, hop, skip, gather nuts, etc. and then at a signal the squirrels have to run home to their nest (any tree).
5. Remember to switch roles (i.e. change the number for the squirrel).

105

Guess My Identity

Primary
Junior
Intermediate
Senior

Group Size: whole class working in pairs

Time Line: 3 minutes

Equipment Needed: none

Space Required: classroom

Activity Description:

1. Each person in the group takes on an identity different than his/her own. (animal, community helper etc.)
2. Partner up.
3. Ask partner to guess what animal he/she is by using 3 questions only. Yes or no answers. i.e. Are you a reptile? Are you a meat-eater? etc.

Purple Stew

Primary
Junior
Intermediate
Senior

Group Size: whole class

Time Line: flexible

Equipment Needed: piano or keyboard (if available)

Space Required: open area

Activity Description:

1. In circle formation sing Purple Stew.
2. Person in the middle points to another at the end of the song.
3. Goal: To have everyone have a chance to be in the middle (stirring)
4. Singing is a positive and fun experience.
5. Possibility for add-ons - e.g. change colour ingredients, etc.

Purple Stew

Making a Purple Stew (whip whip whip) (stirring action)
Making a Purple Stew (Scoo Be Doo Be With)
Purple Potatoes and Purple Tomatoes
And even a purple You ...
Fancy meeting *You* in a purple stew.
(turn around and point to next person to be in stew)

What's This Got To Do With Anything • Jim Craigen & Chris Ward
Kagan Publishing • 1 (800) 933-2667 • www.KaganOnline.com

Walking Chant

Group Size: small to larger groups

Time Line: short amount of time - 1-3 minutes

Equipment Needed: none

Space Required: hall, gym, room

Activity Description:

1. When students walk to another area (i.e. classroom to library), have them march in a rhythm.
2. As they march quietly, recite the names of the week or months of the year as practice.
3. Prior to that, students can line up by birth month as you sing "All in together kids, such fine weather kids, get your hat and get your coat. Tell your mother you won't be back til" January, February, etc.

If You Like... (Skip to My Lou music)

Group Size: whole class

Time Line: 10 minutes

Equipment Needed: none

Space Required: open

Activity Description:

1. Sing "Skip to My Lou". Add verses to song:

   "If you like peaches stand right up.
   If you like peaches turn around.
   If you like peaches sit back down.
   Skip to my Lou my darling."

2. Add anything in verses: "If you have blue eyes"; "If you like recess".

107

Career Matching

Primary
Junior
Intermediate
Senior

Group Size: whole class divided into 4's

Time Line: 5 minutes

Equipment Needed: none

Space Required: classroom with open space or gymnasium

Activity Description:

1. This activity would be used as an introduction to the "community helpers" theme in primary grades.
2. On chart paper, teacher will list various occupations which help others in the community.
3. In an envelope, there will be various pieces of paper with these jobs printed on them ... one occupation per piece of paper with these jobs printed on them (i.e. firefighter, nurse, doctor, policeperson, teacher, etc.).
4. Each student will receive one piece of paper.
5. Individuals will silently act out their specific career and match up with other students sharing identical careers.
* This is an enjoyable method by which to match students! (Good energizer and group former!)

Donut Colour Game

Primary
Junior
Intermediate
Senior

Group Size: whole group

Time Line: as long as interest is there

Equipment Needed: cut out donuts with colour words on them

Space Required: circle

Activity Description:

1. Students gather in a group and recite the following poem:

Down around the corner at the bakery shop
There were 10 little donuts with sugar on top
Along came (name of child) all alone
and he/she took a (child chooses a donut
and says the name of the colour) one home

2. As poem is recited, the named child walks around the circle, grabs the donut and then finds place in circle to sit.
3. Person without the donut becomes "it."

What's This Got To Do With Anything • Jim Craigen & Chris Ward
Kagan Publishing • 1 (800) 933-2667 • www.KaganOnline.com

Rhythm Patterns

Group Size: whole class or smaller groups

Time Line: 5 minutes

Equipment Needed: none - just students

Space Required: carpet area to sit in circle

Activity Description:

1. Everyone sits in one large circle (this activity could also be done in smaller groups).
2. One person begins by demonstrating a rhythm, i.e. clap twice, hands on knees, snap fingers, etc.
3. Individuals add on to the pattern and the group, as a whole, tries to remember the entire pattern.

Primary
Junior
Intermediate
Senior

Shoulder-to-Shoulder

Group Size: any

Time Line: 30 seconds - 2 minutes

Equipment Needed: none

Space Required: enough space in classroom for each student to move slightly

Activity Description:

1. Students get into any size group (for younger students, have same sex groups).
2. Call out part of body, i.e. hand.
3. Every member has to touch each other's same body part with that body part (i.e. hand to hand or shoulder to shoulder or elbow to elbow, etc.)

Primary
Junior
Intermediate
Senior

109

Between Inning Stretch

Group Size: whole class

Time Line: 1-5 minutes

Equipment Needed: none

Space Required: classroom

Activity Description:

1. Students and teachers recite the following and perform actions.

Touch your nose, touch your toes. See how far your fingers grow.
(Stretch with arms at full extension, as are fingers.)

2. Mix up instructions, e.g. nose, toes, nose, toes, fingers grow ...

Group Listening Activity – "The Little Old Man"

Group Size: whole class

Time Line: 3-5 minutes

Equipment Needed: none (story attached – see following page.)

Space Required: classroom

Activity Description:

1. Divide class into 4 groups.
2. Assign each group to stand and make a particular sound when it hears its cue words.

Cue Words	Sounds
tire	whirr, whirr
windshield wipers	swish, swish
horn	honk, honk
engine	vroom, vroom

What's This Got To Do With Anything • Jim Craigen & Chris Ward
Kagan Publishing • 1 (800) 933-2667 • www.KaganOnline.com

The Little Old Man

Primary
Junior
Intermediate
Senior

Not too long ago, there lived a little old man. His house was quite a distance from town. Whenever he needed groceries, the little old man had to walk several miles to the nearest store. One day, the little old man's shopping took longer than usual. It was nearly dusk before he began his long journey home.

The little old man had walked about a mile when he came upon four tires in the road. The little old man thought it strange that someone would leave four tires in the middle of the road, but he continued toward home. Behind him, he could hear the tires going **whirr, whirr.**

As the little old man approached a grove of trees, he noticed a pair of windshield wipers caught on a tree branch. The night breeze jiggled the windshield wipers. The windshield wipers caught on a tree branch. The night breeze jiggled the windshield wipers. The windshield wipers went **swish, swish.** The little old man hurried past the windshield wipers and whispered to himself that he was not afraid. But behind him he could hear the tires going **whirr, whirr,** and the windshield wipers going **swish, swish.**

Rounding a bend in the road, the little old man came upon a horn. The horn was going **honk, honk.** The little old man began to run. Behind him, he could hear the tires going **whirr, whirr,** the windshield wipers going **swish, swish,** and the horn going **honk, honk.**

The little old man kept telling himself he was not afraid. His house was a short distance away. As he ran toward the front door, he tripped over a car engine. The engine was going **vroom, vroom.**

"What is going on?" asked the little old man. "I've walked by four tires going **whirr, whirr,** a pair of windshield wipers going **swish, swish,** a horn going **honk, honk** and now there's an engine in my front yard going **vroom, vroom.** Well, maybe I can put all of this junk to good use." With that thought in mind, the little old man went to his garage. He got out some tools and began tinkering.

At sunrise the little old man stopped. In front of him stood a contraption that resembled a car. It was made out of odds and ends and the car parts that had followed him home.

"Now, let's drive to town," said the little old man. As he drove down the road, you could hear four tires going **whirr, whirr,** a pair of windshield wipers going **swish, swish,** a horn going **honk, honk,** an engine going **vroom, vroom,** and a little old man laughing.

What's This Got To Do With Anything • Jim Craigen & Chris Ward
Kagan Publishing • 1 (800) 933-2667 • www.KaganOnline.com

This Is My ...

Primary
Junior
Intermediate
Senior

Group Size: whole class

Time Line: 10 minutes

Equipment Needed: none

Space Required: enough room to have students form a circle

This is my knee

Activity Description:

1. With the teacher and students standing in a circle, a person begins by pointing to a part of their body (e.g. eye) and saying, "This is my elbow."
2. The next person points to their elbow and says another body part (i.e. knee).
3. The first time around the circle they will go slowly and then you speed it up until everyone collapses in laughter. Yes, you can reuse body parts.

The Surprise

Primary
Junior
Intermediate
Senior

Group Size: groups of 3 or 4

Time Line: 10 minutes

Equipment Needed: one gift-wrapped box with any item (unknown to class) inside, writing paper, pencils

Space Required: enough space for groups of 3 or 4 people to be comfortable writing

Activity Description:

1. Brainstorm - as a whole group question what might be inside box.
2. Children in groups make a list of objects that could be hidden in box. (Roles - reader/recorder; materials manager; praiser.)
3. Share ideas in whole group.
4. Open the "gift"

Follow-up "brainstorm" (possibly for next day) - from home children bring in a surprise item that's gift-wrapped for their small group to guess what's inside.

112

A-Hunting We Will Go

Group Size: any size over 15

Time Line: 5-10 minutes

Equipment Needed: none

Space Required: gym or classroom

Activity Description:

1. Two people join hands and make a bridge by raising hands above head.
2. Rest of the members form a line at one side of bridge.
3. At the beginning of the song the line moves under the bridge to the other side and after the entire line goes through the leader of the line continues through the bridge again.
4. At the point in song - on the word "catch" - bridge falls (arms) down catching the fox or foxes.
5. The caught foxes join the bridge and game continues until the remaining foxes are caught.

Keep The Kettle Boiling

Group Size: whole class

Time Line: variable

Equipment Needed: any medium sized object (one)

Space Required: enough for a class circle

Activity Description:

1. All students sit in a circle.
2. Leader with object must (without speaking) choose another to pass the object to.
3. He/she then takes that person's place in the circle.
4. The new object holder must then choose someone else to pass the object to.
5. No one must speak.
6. Object is to never let one person touch or possess the object twice.
7. Students must concentrate on who has already had the object so when their turn arrives they'll know who can still get it.
8. Game ends when someone tries to give the object to a previous possessor.

113

Pass The Clap I

Group Size: any size

Time Line: 5 minutes

Equipment Needed: none

Space Required: enough for your group to stand in a complete circle

Activity Description:

1. All stand in a circle facing in.
2. As a leader, turn to your right and "take a clap" from that person → to do this, open your hands and you and that person clap hands together.
3. When you have received this clap, turn and pass it to the person on your left.
4. There should only be one clapping sound. (Your hands make contact at the same time.)
5. This continues around the circle → begin slow then speed it up.
6. Soon it will be "flipping" around the circle.

This is not as difficult as it sounds - just hard to put on paper. When it gets going fast, it looks really neat; kids really like it! For variety, change directions and see if they can still do it.

Pass the Clap II

Group Size: whole class

Time Line: until saturation or 10-15 minutes

Equipment Needed:

Space Required: classroom, gym

Activity Description:

1. In circle formation, teacher leads clap pattern 1, 2, 3, 4.
2. On 4, the teacher does a double clap and passes it to student on right.
3. Student then follows the same pattern and passes again to his right.

Variations:
Instead of double clap on "beat 4", make eye contact instead (wink, blink), pass other clap forms (behind back, under leg).

What's This Got To Do With Anything • Jim Craigen & Chris Ward
Kagan Publishing • 1 (800) 933-2667 • www.KaganOnline.com

What Monster?

Group Size: class size or smaller

Time Line: varies

Equipment Needed: space - people

Space Required: clear area to stand in a circle

Activity Description:

1. Arrange everyone in a circle.
2. Turn the "it" person from facing inward to facing side profile.
3. The "it" sends the message to the person on his/her right using body and voice saying, "What Monster?".
4. The next person jumps and turns to the next person and copies the body language exactly.
5. The same message is sent around.
6. When the message returns to the original "sender" the person changes his/her body to answer the question - "This Monster" and the message flows through the circle in reverse, jumping and changing direction as your body answers.
7. When the answer reaches the person who originally asked "What Monster?" the next person to this individual starts the game again.

Hello Friend

Group Size: two to three groups, size dependent on class size

Time Line: 10 minutes

Equipment Needed: none

Space Required: classroom

Activity Description:

1. Form a circle and choose one person to start.
2. Decide on a silent form of greeting; greeting must be passed on one by one around the circle.
3. Those who laugh or smile must sit in centre of circle.
4. Those who are in centre can try silently to make others laugh so they have to join them.
5. After first greeting has gone around then another student starts a greeting.
6. Continue until everyone is in middle or has had a turn to start a greeting - whichever happens first.

115

Magic Squeeze

Group Size: whole class or class divided into 2

Time Line: 2-3 minutes

Equipment Needed: none

Space Required: enough to make a circle

Activity Description:

1. Group makes circle.
2. Hold hands.
3. One participant stands in middle.
4. Leader silently sends magic squeeze (i.e. squeezes partner's hand) around circle.
5. Each receiver sends it on in same fashion.
6. Person in centre watches for direction the squeeze is sent in and points to any receiver.
7. If the squeezer is identified before sending the squeeze on, switch places.

Musical Statues

Group Size: small group to full class size

Time Line: 10 minutes

Equipment Needed: "Music Maker" - tape player, etc. or keyboard (preferable)

Space Required: open space is better but classroom setting can work

Activity Description:

1. Like musical chairs except that when the music stops the students must "freeze".
2. Last one to freeze is out.
3. If done with groups, they can cheer their teammates on.
4. Can also be done as groups.
5. Members of a group could hold hands, link arms, etc.
6. Last group to "freeze" is out.
7. This would have fewer students sitting for a "long" time.

116

Barnyard Choral Society's "Good King Wensceslas"

Group Size: any size over 10; more = better

Time Line: 10 minutes maximum

Equipment Needed: voices

Space Required: horseshoe formation

Activity Description:

1. Three groups: group #1 = cows "moo"; #2 = sheep "bhaa bhaa"; #3 = pigs "oink".
2. Using tune to "Good King Wensceslas", each group substitutes barnyard sound for lyrics.
3. The teacher is conductor.
4. Singers only respond to hand signals.
5. Hence, sounds could be - bhaa, bhaa, moo, moo, bhaa, oink, bhaa.
6. You can fool groups by looking at cows while pointing to sheep.
7. Good for eye contact and following directions.

Food Chain/Word Train

Group Size: any size

Time Line: any predetermined time

Equipment Needed: none

Space Required: large enough for circle

Activity Description:

1. Task/Goal - choose topic - food, countries, sports, careers, etc.
2. First person names a food, the next person adds a food that begins with the last letter of the previously named food.

Person A says appl**e**
Person B says eg**g**
Person C says grape**s**

117

Grocery Chain

Group Size: 20-30

Time Line: flexible

Equipment Needed: none

Space Required: room enough to make a group circle

Activity Description:

1. Leader begins with "Mrs. Cow went to the store and bought *butter*."
2. She fills in an item and it passes on to the next person who must add to this, e.g. "Mrs. Cow went to the store and bought butter and an egg."
3. Continue around the group adding onto the chain and trying not to "break" it.
4. Whole group joins in with chanting of the chain.

It Is Not "I"

Group Size: class

Time Line: 5-10 minutes

Equipment Needed: chalk

Space Required: classroom

Activity Description:

1. Students are told to put heads down, close eyes and hold one hand open.
2. Teacher or student walks around and places chalk in a student's hand.
3. Keeps walking.
4. Teacher says "Hands closed, eyes open, heads up."
5. One person starts by selecting another child who they think has the chalk.
6. Child says "It is not I" until the correct child has been called.
7. Keep the score of guesses.

What's This Got To Do With Anything • Jim Craigen & Chris Ward
Kagan Publishing • 1 (800) 933-2667 • www.KaganOnline.com

Clapping Game

Group Size: whole class

Time Line: 2-3 minutes

Equipment Needed: anything found in the classroom

Space Required: group at front of room

Activity Description:

1. Send one student out of the room.
2. As a group, decide on an object that you want that child to pick up in the room.
3. Ask the student to come back into the room.
4. The group claps softly and then gradually louder as the student approaches the object to be picked up.
5. The idea is to use the volume of clapping to solve the problem.

Hide, Seek and Clap

Group Size: classroom

Time Line: 10 minutes

Equipment Needed: a small object such as a thimble, paper clip etc.

Space Required: classroom

Activity Description:

1. Hold up the small object and choose three players to leave the room while you and others decide where to hide it.
2. When it's hidden, invite the three to come back and work together to find it.
3. The rest of the group claps softly to a steady beat, clapping loudly when any of the three players get close to the object. (No talking or gesturing.)
4. After the three players find the object, they each select a new player for the next round of "Hide, Seek and Clap".

119

What's This Got To Do With Anything • Jim Craigen & Chris Ward
Kagan Publishing • 1 (800) 933-2667 • www.KaganOnline.com

Here Comes The Teacher

Primary
Junior
Intermediate
Senior

Group Size: whole class

Time Line: 5-10 minutes

Equipment Needed: chairs in a circle

Space Required: centre space in a class-room

Activity Description:

1. Students, except one who is the story-teller, sit in their chairs. Have one less chair than number of students.
2. The storyteller walks around the room telling a story that he/she has made up.
3. Suddenly he/she says "The teacher's coming".
4. On this cue, all students must change seats, and the storyteller must find a seat.
5. The student who remains standing after all have found a seat becomes the new storyteller.

Upset the Fruit Basket

Primary
Junior
Intermediate
Senior

Group Size: any size

Time Line: 5 minutes

Equipment Needed: chairs

Space Required: class

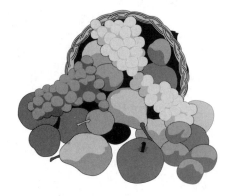

Activity Description:

1. Assign all students a number.
2. All students sit on chairs but one stands within circle formed by chairs.
3. Student standing calls out two or more numbers.
4. Students whose numbers are called change seats, including the standing person who was "it".
5. Students whose numbers are called cannot go to the seat they left.
6. The standing person then becomes it and repeats step 3 again.
7. For all students to change you call "Upset the Fruit Basket".

120

Brainstorming Activity

Group Size: whole class

Time Line: 5 minutes

Equipment Needed: ABC letters or theme cards (apple, Hallowe'en, winter)

Space Required: classroom, groups of 4 in desks

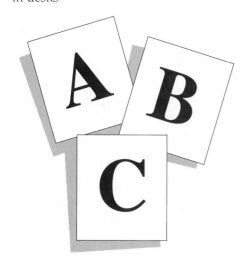

Activity Description:

1. Students are in small groups.
2. Student #1 takes a letter card and brainstorms as many words as possible that begin with that letter.
3. When he/she runs out of words, pass the card to Student #2.
4. Student #2 continues and then passes card to #3.
5. Each time the card is passed, count silently 1 steamboat, 2 steamboat, 3 steamboat; if the card holder has not come up with a word, pass card.
6. Student #4 tallies the number of words.
7. Start again with #3 recording etc.
8. Try to beat the previous score.

The More We Get Together

Group Size: any size group divided into 3

Time Line: 5 minutes

Equipment Needed: none

Space Required: classroom

Activity Description:

1. Divide whole group into 3 subgroups.

Group 1: goes "Um-Sh-Sh/Um-Sh-Sh" as they squat momentarily, then rise with arms extended, punching twice as they say Sh-Sh.

Group 2: goes "Um-Deedley-dee/Um-Deedley-dee" in a high voice.

Group 3: sings The More We Get Together, together, together, etc.

2. All 3 groups do this together.
3. Usually it brings laughter with inhibitions breaking down.

121

Music

Primary
Junior
Intermediate
Senior

Group Size: whole class

Time Line: 3 minutes

Equipment Needed: song: Scotland's Burning

Space Required: small section of room

Activity Description:

1. The song "Scotland's Burning" is very easy to learn.
2. Children stand in circle.
3. Sing and do actions:

*Scotland's Burning, Scotland's Burning -
point fingers out of a circle
Fire - Fire - Fire - Fire - jump up and down
Water - Water - Water - Water - pour water
Hose it down - Hose it down - bend down
and stand straight up*

4. You may increase the speed of the song as the actions go faster.

Guess the Shape

Primary
Junior
Intermediate
Senior

Group Size: whole class in partners

Time Line: 5-10 minutes

Equipment Needed: paper bags, 3 dimensional shapes

Space Required: classroom

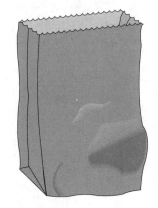

Activity Description:

1. 1st child closes his/her eyes.
2. 2nd child puts shape into paper bag.
3. 1st child puts his/her hand into bag to feel the shape and tries to guess what it is.

(In junior grades, they can ask questions, i.e. "How many vertices, edges?")

122

Bumpety-Bump-Bump

Group Size: whole class

Time Line: 5 minutes

Equipment Needed: none

Space Required: large enough for a circle

Activity Description:

1. Form a circle standing up with a chosen "it" in the centre.
2. The "it" walks up to you and stands in front of you and says one of the following:

Centre, (pause) *bumpety-bump-bump.*
Self, (pause) *bumpety-bump-bump.*
Right, (pause) *bumpety-bump-bump.*
Left, (pause) *bumpety-bump-bump.*

3. The person in the circle must say his/her own name (centre), or "it's" name (self), or the person's name to the right or left of him/her before "it" completes saying "bumpety-bump-bump", otherwise he/she becomes "it".

Variation:
Scramble the circle and begin again.

Let's Estimate-10-second Count

Group Size: whole class

Time Line: 5 minutes

Equipment Needed: paper, pencil

Space Required: desk

Activity Description:

1. Students fold paper in 8.
2. In first left box write 10 seconds (for example) and f.s. (finger snap).
3. Child estimates how many times they can snap fingers in 10 seconds and records the number in the first box.
4. Then ready-go they count how many times they can snap in 10 seconds and record in box beside the first box.
5. Amazement sets in. Do one more time for more realistic estimate.
6. Could also use tongue snaps, claps or blinks.
7. Ask how many with less than 10, less than 20, over 40.
8. Results are non-threatening. They love the guess work.

123

Rescue

Group Size: class

Time Line: flexible

Equipment Needed: taped music (or keyboard), double sheet newspapers torn into island shapes that hold a certain number of students (e.g. six).

Space Required: large enough for class to make a circle

Activity Description:

1. Class forms circle.
2. Newspaper Islands inside and outside circle.
3. Pretend room is an ocean.
4. Everyone in his/her own canoe - rowing and moving slowly around in circle as music plays.
5. Stop music: Yell "Shipwreck".
6. Everyone "swims" to an island and helps others onto island until six on each.
7. Must have both feet on island.
8. Repeat as often as time or interest allows.
9. Tear islands so only 4 kids fit on. Repeat.
10. Tear islands so only 3 fit on.
11. These are your groups. Adapt island sizes and numbers to fit your class size.

Frog and Fly

Group Size: 20-30

Time Line: 10-15 minutes

Equipment Needed: nothing but a blindfold

Space Required: gymnasium/classroom

Activity Description:

1. Students are in a circle.
2. One frog is blindfolded and inside the circle, and there is one fly inside the circle also.
3. Object is for frog to catch the fly by tracking the sound of the fly's voice.
4. Fly says "Buzz, buzz" in response to the frog's words "Croak, croak".
5. Players in circle makes sounds of the wind by humming or saying "Oooh, oooh".
6. The fly is not allowed to run.
7. When caught, the fly becomes a frog and frog chooses a new fly.
8. Have fun!

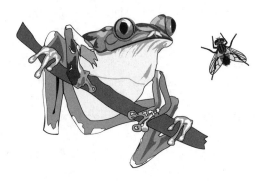

What's This Got To Do With Anything • Jim Craigen & Chris Ward
Kagan Publishing • 1 (800) 933-2667 • www.KaganOnline.com

Speed Counting in French or English

Group Size: whole class

Time Line: 20-30 seconds

Equipment Needed: voices, knowledge of numbers 1-10

Space Required: class, groups - can be done as a timed activity for groups

Activity Description:

1. Rapid counting from #1-10 in French or English.
2. Vary instructions as follows:

Plus doucement	*More softly*
Plus fort	*(Louder) → More loudly*
Plus vite (plus rapidement)	*(Faster) → More quickly*
Plus lentement	*More slowly*

1 2 3 4 5 6 7 8 9 10

Inside/Outside

Group Size: whole class

Time Line: 8-10 minutes

Equipment Needed: animal picture cards - enough for 1/2 the class and title cards - "Items", "Food", "Enemies", covering enough for 1/2 the class

Space Required: 1/4 of room

Activity Description:

1. Form a circle within a circle, children from one facing the other circle.
2. Have the children in the inner circle each have a picture card. (animal)
3. Have the children in the outer circle with a title card.
4. Have the children move.
5. They must tell about the animal according to the titlecard, e.g. beaver → home = dam, etc.

Variation:
Switch cards. Move children on the inside circle around.

Hint:
If numbers are uneven, teacher joins one circle or two children pair up.

125

Build a Story

Group Size: whole class

Time Line: 20 minutes

Equipment Needed: squares of construction paper (15 cm) with a symbol drawn on each (one for each participant), i.e. tree, star, cup and saucer, house, etc.)

Space Required: students need to sit together in a circle

Activity Description:

1. To begin, pass the cards out to all the students face down.
2. Instruct the students not to look at them until they are told.
3. Select a student to begin a story by turning over their own symbol card and including that symbol or its meaning into their story.
4. Following this, the person to the story teller's left takes over the story, and turns over their symbol ready to include that concept or symbol in the story.
5. When the story reaches the last person, he/she must end the story including their symbol.

Gum Relay

Group Size: small groups

Time Line: depends on age - younger students need more time

Equipment Needed: large pair of men's gloves - 1 pair per group, 1 package gum (like Wrigley's) per group

Space Required: 10-20 feet (for relay)

Activity Description:

1. Each group lines up single file behind line.
2. At command, 1st person in line runs to gloves and gum; puts on gloves; takes out a piece of gum; puts it in mouth; throws wrapper in garbage; takes off gloves and returns to group to set off next person.
3. Everyone wins (gets a piece of gum) and yet this contains an element of competition and group building.

Variation:
This can also be done with sugarless candies wrapped in a wrapper and placed in a bag.

126

Twist and Touch

Group Size: partners

Time Line: 3-5 minutes

Equipment Needed: none

Space Required: each group of 2 needs approximately one square meter of space

Activity Description:

1. Partners face each other and hold a hand.
2. Each person does a complete turn inside out (don't let go) and touch the floor with your joined hands, on the right side.
3. Twist again and touch the left.
4. Twist and touch right, etc.
5. Continue until you master.
6. Try new partner every time.

Wink Mixer

Group Size: whole class

Time Line: 15 minutes

Equipment Needed: chairs for half of the people

Space Required: large

Activity Description:

1. One half of students sit in chairs in circle - other half stand behind each chair.
2. One chair is empty with someone standing behind it.
3. The person behind the empty chair winks at some person in a chair.
4. That person runs to sit in the winker's chair.
5. Then the person without a partner winks to new person.
6. If you don't want to lose your partner you can hold the sitting person's shoulders so he/she can't run away and the winker has to wink at someone else.

127

Graph-it!

Group Size: whole class

Time Line: 10-20 minutes

Equipment Needed: students, graph-grid outlined with tape on floor

Space Required: open area - floor space (the usual 'meeting place' in a primary room)

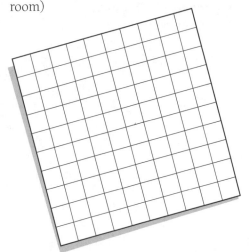

Activity Description:

1. Tell students they are to try to make a co-operative graph.
2. Name graphing item, i.e. "SHOES".
3. Each child takes off 1 shoe.
4. Group by group students come to graph on floor and place shoe in appropriate column - SILENTLY.
5. The first group will define columns by how they place shoe. (i.e. velcro, lace, slip on, canvas, patent, etc.)
6. Children coming to graph will need to silently discover (1) graph sorting and (2) place shoe appropriately.
7. After graph is completed, discuss graph columns, # of each type (re: more/less), and how else could we have graphed.

Syllable Symphony

Group Size: any number

Time Line: 30 seconds/round

Equipment Needed: none

Space Required: nothing special - can be done seated or standing

Activity Description:

1. Divide group into 3 sections.
2. One person leaves the room.
3. Decide on a 3 syllable word (i.e. happiness)
4. Each group chants 1 syllable simultaneously - Group 1: *"Hap Hap Hap..."*,
Group 2: *"E E E..."*, Group 3: *"Ness Ness Ness..."*.
5. The person who left returns and must figure out the word.

Hap Hap Hap...

What's This Got To Do With Anything • Jim Craigen & Chris Ward
Kagan Publishing • 1 (800) 933-2667 • www.KaganOnline.com

Story Builder

Group Size: 5 and up

Time Line: 10-15 minutes

Equipment Needed: bean bag

Space Required: room to make a circle

Activity Description:

1. The students are given a starting line of a story (this can relate to a theme, etc.).
2. The bean bag is then handed to student who continues the story by adding a sentence.
3. When finished, the student tosses the bean bag to another student in the circle.
4. This person adds a line.
5. This process continues until each student has had a turn or the story is complete.

Circle Dodge Ball

Group Size: whole class

Time Line: five minutes

Equipment Needed: large ball

Space Required: space for a large circle

Activity Description:

1. To play this game, have players form two circles, one inside the other.
2. Players in the inside circle join hands and walk around clockwise.
3. The players in the outside circle roll a large ball across the circle and try to hit the legs of a player on the inside circle.
4. When the ball makes contact with a player, he or she joins the outside circle and continues to play.
5. Players in the inside circle may jump or run to avoid the ball, but they must not let go of each other's hands.
6 The game is over when all the players from the inside circle have joined the outside circle.

129

Change 5

Group Size: whole class

Time Line: 5 minutes

Equipment Needed: none

Space Required: open space in classroom

Activity Description:

1. Students form inside/outside circle.
2. Outside people move 4 spaces to the right to find their partner.
3. Welcome one another.
4. Students "study" (observe) one another carefully.
5. After a given time, students turn around, change 5 things about themselves (i.e. unbutton shirt, take off glasses, etc.).
6. Students then pair up again and try to identify the changes.

Look Twice

Group Size: whole class

Time Line: 1-2 minutes

Equipment Needed: none

Space Required: minimal

Activity Description:

1. Have 1 student stand in front of the class while the rest observe what he/she is wearing.
2. All students close their eyes while the model changes one aspect of dress.
3. Students guess the change.
4. Good activity when students are dressed for home.

What's This Got To Do With Anything • Jim Craigen & Chris Ward
Kagan Publishing • 1 (800) 933-2667 • www.KaganOnline.com

I'm Going On A Trip

Group Size: 10-30

Time Line: approximately 10 minutes

Equipment Needed: a ball

Space Required: open space; students stand in a circle

Activity Description:

1. Students stand in a circle and one student is given a ball.
2. He says "I'm going on a trip today and I'm putting on a warm sweater". (He acts it out.)
3. Ball is tossed to another student.
4. Second student might say "I'm going on a trip today and I'm putting on a warm sweater and carrying a heavy suitcase". (He acts it out.)
5. If a player can't repeat instruction, he must pass to another student.

Primary
Junior
Intermediate
Senior

"Oh Deer" (from Project Wild)

Group Size: 10-60

Time Line: approximately 5-40 minutes

Equipment Needed: none

Space Required: varies depending on size of group: outside or inside (classroom with desks cleared or gymnasium)

Activity Description:

1. Cooperative game involving students being designated as a deer "A" line or what the deer needs to live (shelter, food or water) "B" line.
2. Two lines face opposite direction, everyone in the "B" line choosing whether they will be food, shelter or water.
3. The deer then decide and indicate which element they need to survive.
4. Players cannot change their signs until each round is over.
5. Upon the whistle sounded by leader (teacher), the 2 lines turn around facing each other.
6. The deer go to the other side to retrieve what they need.
7. If they don't get it, they become an element and the game continues another round.

Primary
Junior
Intermediate
Senior

131

Funny Face

Primary
Junior
Intermediate
Senior

Group Size: groups of 3 or 4

Time Line: 5 minutes

Equipment Needed: paper (1/person), clock with second hand or egg timer, markers - 5 different colours (1/person)

Space Required: one table/group, one chair/person

Activity Description:

1. Each child draws an oval on page (10 seconds time limit).
2. Pass pages to the left.
3. Each child adds eyes (15 seconds) → pass to left.
4. Each child adds nose (15 seconds) → pass to left.
5. Each child adds ears (15 seconds) → pass to left.
6. Each child adds hair (15 seconds) → pass to left.
   ...and so on until faces are complete.

All Wound Up

Primary
Junior
Intermediate
Senior

Group Size: 25

Time Line: 10 minutes

Equipment Needed: tape recorder, music

Space Required: large area

Activity Description:

1. Choose a favourite song that players can sing with gusto and make a circle with everyone holding hands.
2. Leader drops left hand and while singing, slowly leads the players clockwise around the inside of the circle.
3. When the leader reaches the centre of the circle he/she ducks slightly and passes under the arms of players on one radius of the coil, moving from the centre out.
4. As the leader pulls the line of players with him/her, those still in the coil arch arms to let the line through.
5. As everyone passes through the arch, the coil unwinds into a straight line.
6. When you're all unwound, make your original circle, end your song and take a bow!

What's This Got To Do With Anything • Jim Craigen & Chris Ward
Kagan Publishing • 1 (800) 933-2667 • www.KaganOnline.com

Human Tic Tac Toe

Primary
Junior
Intermediate
Senior

Group Size: whole class divided into 2 or 4 groups

Time Line: 10-15 minutes

Equipment Needed: post-it notes

Space Required: classroom or gym

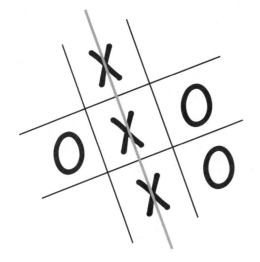

Activity Description:

1. Divide group into two teams (or four smaller teams for greater interaction).
2. Give each team one colour of paper to stick to their shirts.
3. Post it notes are great.
4. Children number off.
5. Set up 9 chairs in 3 rows of 3.
6. Act as or appoint a caller.
7. Caller says a number such as 5.
8. No. 5 players sit down in any 2 chairs as quickly as possible.
9. Game continues until 3 players from the same team score a "tic-tac-toe".
10. If tac toe toe doesn't happen and all seats are taken, start again.

Odd or Even

Primary
Junior
Intermediate
Senior

Group Size: pairs

Time Line: 5 minutes

Equipment Needed: 10 beans for each pair of players

Space Required: minimal

Activity Description:

This game was played in ancient Greece and can be used to reinforce math skills.

1. Divide players into pairs and give each player ten beans.
2. To begin, one player from each pair puts some beans in one hand, closes it, and holds it out toward his or her opponent.
3. "Odd or even?" asks the first player.
4. The opposing player looks at the closed fist and makes a guess, either "odd" or "even".
5. If the guesser is correct, he or she takes one bean from the opposing player.
6. If the guesser is incorrect, he or she forfeits one bean to the opposing player.
7. Players take turns guessing and hiding beans until one of the players has no more beans.

133

Sousa Jive

Primary
Junior
Intermediate
Senior

Group Size: whole class or smaller groups

Time Line: 4-5 minutes

Equipment Needed: tape deck or record player, recorded Sousa March (Liberty Bell, Washington Post)

Space Required: students can participate at their desks; just stand up and step back from desk

Activity Description:

1. Jive: (a) slap knees twice, (b) clap hands twice, (c) left hand over right hand twice, (d) right hand over left hand twice, (e) snap on right side twice, (f) snap on left side twice, (g) thumb up on right side twice "hitch", (h) thumb up on left side twice.

Note:
Marches have ABA form - reverse jive pattern in the B Section.
Also, wait for the short introduction before beginning Jive.

Sing-a-long Math

Primary
Junior
Intermediate
Senior

Group Size: class (in small groups)

Time Line: 5 minutes

Equipment Needed: voices!

Space Required: classroom

3, 6, 9, 12

Activity Description:

1. Using multiples (3, 6, 9, 12, etc.), (7, 14, 21, 28, etc.), etc., have the small groups sing them to a familiar tune.
2. Practise and present to the class and the class sings along.

Note:
At Christmas we used Christmas carols - they loved it.

134

Telephone

Group Size: whole class

Time Line: 5 minutes

Equipment Needed: none

Space Required: classroom

Activity Description:

1. Children can stand in a line or remain at their desks.
2. Teacher gives one student a single sentence.
3. The student whispers the sentence into ear of student next to him/her.
4. They continue to pass the phrase along to the last in the row.
5. That student now says phrase to all repeating what he/she heard.

The Great Kapok Tree *by Lynne Cherry*

Group Size: 10 and up

Time Line: 10 to 15 minutes

Equipment Needed: the book called *The Great Kapok Tree*, markers, construction paper, and a tape recorder

Space Required: this energizer can be done in a small or large space

Activity Description:

1. This story is a good introduction to a unit on the environment.
2. Write out the parts of the animals on construction paper.
3. Have the students practise the sounds of the animals in the story.
4. The narrator reads the introduction.
5. When the narrator finishes reading about an animal, the students representing this animal read their part.
6. Once the student (or students) has completed the part, the class makes the sound of that animal.
7. At the end of the story the students make the sound of the animal that they are in the story.
8. This makes it sound like there is a forest in the class.
9. You may want to record the class so that they can hear all of the sounds.

135

Shell Game

Primary
Junior
Intermediate
Senior

Group Size: math class

Time Line: varies

Equipment Needed: calculators

Space Required: classroom

Activity Description:

1. Task: Have students try to spell the word "shell" on their calculators.
2. Hint: Numbers of the desired word must be in reverse order, i.e. 77345. Turn the calculator upside down to read the word.
3. You can make it difficult by telling them to spell the name of a popular gas station on their calculators, i.e. 0553

0 = O	5 = S
1 = I	6 = G
2 = Z	7 = L
3 = E	8 = B
4 = H	9 = G

4. The numbers on a calculator will display as the above letters when the calculator is turned upside down.
5. Have children make up own riddles or equations to get a "word" answer.
i.e. 1010 - 202 = a man's name that is the same backwards and forwards. i.e. BOB.

Star Formation

Primary
Junior
Intermediate
Senior

Group Size: whole class

Time Line: 5 minutes

Equipment Needed: none

Space Required: a lot

Activity Description:

1. Hold hands in a large circle and number off "1, 2 .. 1, 2 .. 1, 2 ..."
2. At the instruction "1, 2, 3, lean", all #1's lean in forward and all #2's lean out backwards.
3. Support each other.
4. Instruction: "1, 2, 3, switch".
5. Slowly change your lean (i.e. kids leaning forward now lean backward and vice versa).

136

Two Behind

Primary
Junior
Intermediate
Senior

Group Size: any size

Time Line: 5 minutes

Equipment Needed: none

Space Required: enough area to hold group size comfortably

Activity Description:

1. Leader performs simple task (snap fingers) and then changes task (jog on spot).
2. Students follow now 1 action behind (snap fingers).
3. Leader changes to stride jumps.
4. Students change to jogging.
5. Students always do action behind leader.
6. They must follow the sequence of the leader.
7. When students get really great at remembering actions have them following actions 2 behind (leader), 3 behind, etc.

Famous Star

Primary
Junior
Intermediate
Senior

Group Size: pairs

Time Line: 5-10 minutes

Equipment Needed: none

Space Required: classroom

Activity Description:

1. Individuals think of their favourite movie star (or sports hero).
2. Quietly move around the room and through questioning try to find someone else who has the same famous movie star as you.
3. You may have to negotiate to find a movie star you both admire.
4. In your "pair" - prepare a pantomime that would enable the audience to identify the star's name.
5. Pantomimes are performed, audience guesses.

137

Blanket Volleyball

Group Size: whole class divided into teams

Time Line: 20 minutes

Equipment Needed: 2 blankets, 1 volleyball, volleyball net

Space Required: gym - or outdoors

Activity Description:

1. 8 on a team.
2. Hold blanket to use as a carrying tool or a catapult.
3. Group must get volleyball over net.
4. The other group must catch the ball in the blanket and return it.

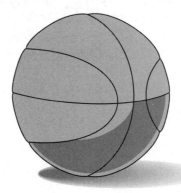

Titles

Group Size: small group

Time Line: 10-15 minutes or task completion

Equipment Needed: "stick-it" papers

Space Required: dependent on number playing

Activity Description:

1. Each student writes the title of a favourite story or book on a "stick-it".
2. "Stick-its" are mixed and 1 is selected by each student.
3. Student places "stick-it" on his/her own forehead or back.
4. Students circulate - each may ask only "yes"/"no" questions until the title they are wearing is identified.

Good energizer and also reviews main ideas of written language. Particularly good for series of anthologies which may have been studied.

138

What's My Sign?

Group Size: any number over 10

Time Line: at least 5 minutes to as long as you want

Equipment Needed: nothing

Space Required: anywhere - standing in circle is great, but can be done at desks

Activity Description:

1. Each person makes up a hand sign.
2. One by one, hand signs are displayed as all watch.
3. They hold their sign until all have displayed theirs.
4. Game begins now.
5. One person (designated starter) shows his/her sign and then someone else's sign.
6. The person who recognizes their sign being displayed flashes their sign and someone else's.
7. This continues.
8. If someone *misses* seeing their sign, you can either end game and start again or that person is out and sits somewhere else (or whatever).
9. Kids love it!

Food Chain Charades

Group Size: any size

Time Line: 20 minutes

Equipment Needed: food chain cards for each student
mouse → rabbit → hawk
grass → deer → wolf
frog → snake → owl
fly → fish → bear

Space Required: open area

Activity Description:

1. Count number of students - divide into threes (if uneven adjust).
2. Mix up animal cards.
3. Give each student a card (don't show anybody).
4. Act out your animal - only sounds allowed are animal sounds.
5. Find someone who might eat you or you might eat.
6. Link arms with members in your food chain.
7. When all animals are linked check your food chain.

139

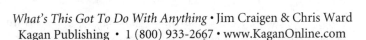

Mental Math

Group Size: individual; small group; whole class

Time Line: about 5 minutes

Equipment Needed: paper, pencil

Activity Description:

1. Select any three digit number in which the digit in the hundreds' place is at least 2 more than the digit in the one's place. (The tens can be any number)
2. Reverse the digits in the ones and hundreds.
3. Subtract #1 and #2 to get a 3rd number.
4. Reverse the digits in the ones and hundreds of the difference to get the 4th number.
5. Add 3 and 4.
6. Result will always be 1089.

803
712
691

Rhythmic Numbers

Group Size: whole class

Time Line: 5 minutes

Equipment Needed: none

Space Required: anywhere in a class

Activity Description:

1. Group size 5-10.
2. Each member in the group numbers himself/herself off (up to the total number in the group).
3. The group begins a slow rhythmic clap.
4. As the clapping begins, one member says his number *plus* the number of another person in the group.
5. This new person says her number plus another number of someone else in the group (without missing a beat).
6. The procedure continues until someone misses their number or beat.
7. Begin procedure again.
8. Increase speed as proficiency allows.

Variation:
Replace numbers with letters, nicknames, names of animals, countries, etc.

What's This Got To Do With Anything • Jim Craigen & Chris Ward
Kagan Publishing • 1 (800) 933-2667 • www.KaganOnline.com

Human Scrabble

Group Size: whole class

Time Line: 10 minutes

Equipment Needed: tags - large and visible with alphabet on them (similar to scrabble tiles but bigger)

Space Required: room

Activity Description:

1. Each student wears or holds a tag.
2. Tags have value on them (as in scrabble).
3. Class has to work to form human chain of words.
4. You can link up perpendicularly or horizontally.
5. After time limit is up, you add the tiles of those who didn't join a word.
6. Class tries to do better next time.

Variation:
Try to do this silently for a change.

What Did You Say?

Group Size: partners

Time Line: 5 minutes

Equipment Needed:

Space Required: minimal

Activity Description:

1. Have students complete the statement "My favourite T.V. show is _____ because _____." or "My favourite team is _____ . because _____."
2. Then have students turn to a neighbour and argue simultaneously that their choice is better.
3. The noise level goes up and it breaks the ice.

What's This Got To Do With Anything • Jim Craigen & Chris Ward
Kagan Publishing • 1 (800) 933-2667 • www.KaganOnline.com

Doctor/Doctor

Group Size: 3 to a group

Time Line: varies

Equipment Needed: 2 pieces of string skipping rope length - butcher cord works best

Space Required: large enough to manoeuvre void of furniture

Activity Description:

1. Have 1 person in group (could be oldest) take or cut 2 pieces of string skipping rope length and tie to wrists of one person in group ensuring that there is a little slack around wrists.
2. The 2nd person ties one wrist then loops the string over partners' string and then ties to his/her other wrist.
3. Now the challenge is for the partners to free each other and get the strings apart.
4. The Doctor's job is to help problem-solve and prevent the pair from becoming entangled.
5. Doctor can untie a wrist to get back to starting position.
6. First group free can go help other groups.

Solution: One player slips the middle of his/her string under the other partner's wrist loop and over the partner's hand.

Mind Reader #1

Group Size: whole class

Time Line: 10 minutes

Equipment Needed: none

Space Required: classroom

Activity Description:

1. Tell students to choose a number between 1-10 but not to tell you what it is.
2. Then tell them that you have an exceptional mind and that you can, after telling them to do a simple math equation, tell them what their answer is.
3. Tell them that, in fact, your mind is so powerful that you will be able to make them all arrive at the same answer if they computed accurately.

Think of your number between 1 and 10 again, but don't tell me what it is. Multiply it by 2. Add 6. Divide by 2. Take away first number you started with. Your answer is 3.

142

Mind Reader #2 (works 95% of the time)

Group Size: whole class

Time Line: 3 minutes

Equipment Needed: none

Space Required: none

Primary
Junior
Intermediate
Senior

Activity Description:

1. Think of a number between 2-9 inclusive.
2. Multiply that number by 9.
3. Add the digits of the product.
4. Subtract 5.
5. Find the corresponding letter of the alphabet, e.g. A = 1, B = 2, etc.
6. Think of a country that starts with that letter.
7. Think of a name of an animal that starts with the 2nd letter of your country but not a bird or a fish.
8. Think of the colour of that animal.

"C'mon, you know there are no grey elephants in Denmark!"

Connect the Dots

Group Size: any size

Time Line: 5-10 minutes (flexible)

Equipment Needed: overhead or handout, put on blackboard

Space Required: regular class

Primary
Junior
Intermediate
Senior

Activity Description:

1. Tell students that they must use only 4 straight lines to connect all 9 dots.
2. Pen cannot leave page.

Question: **Answer:**

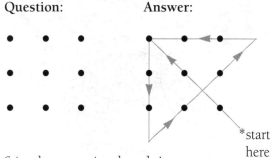

*start here

Stimulates creative thought!

What's This Got To Do With Anything • Jim Craigen & Chris Ward
Kagan Publishing • 1 (800) 933-2667 • www.KaganOnline.com

The Family Name Shuffle

Primary
Junior
Intermediate
Senior

Group Size: the number of families can be adjusted depending on the group size

Time Line: 10 minutes (approximately)

Equipment Needed: cards containing a family name and a position within that family, chairs for each family member with family name on them

Space Required: a fairly large space ... maybe step outside on a nice day

Activity Description:

1. You can choose family names based on a variety of subject areas (i.e. History - great families in history, prime ministers, teachers' names in the school, etc.).
2. If you are using 4 families, set out 4 rows of chairs and label them with the family name.
3. Hand out pre-made cards to each student.
4. Each card will have written on it a family's name and a position within that family (i.e. grandfather, grandmother, father, mother, aunt, son, etc.).
5. Have the students form two circles - a small one within a larger one.
6. Send out commands - inside circle three steps to the right and switch cards.
7. Continue to give commands until all the cards have been nicely *shuffled*.
8. The teacher then says "go" (or maybe something more original) and that is the signal for everyone to find their family chairs and to sit down on the chairs in the family order (i.e. grandfather, then grandmother, then father, then mother, etc. or women first (i.e. grandmother, grandfather, mother, father, etc.).
9. The order must be explained prior to the "go" signal.
10. You can go back to the inside/outside circle to reshuffle the cards and to repeat the activity.
11. The goal is to be the first family sitting in the correct order.
12. The teacher may need to check the order.

What's This Got To Do With Anything • Jim Craigen & Chris Ward
Kagan Publishing • 1 (800) 933-2667 • www.KaganOnline.com

Alphabet - Geography

Group Size: groups of 3 to 6

Time Line: 5 to 10 minutes

Equipment Needed: none

Space Required: chair circle or tables

Activity Description:

1. One person begins and names a geographical place, or landform, e.g. river, city, continent, country.
2. Then the next person names one that starts with the last letter of the previous name, e.g. if first person names "Nile", next person must name one starting with "e" such as Edmonton, then the next turn would begin with "n" and so on.

Who Dunnit?

Group Size: whole class

Time Line: 10 to 15 minutes

Equipment Needed: none

Space Required: regular classroom

Activity Description:

Situation: *A true story:* A guard is making sure everybody is in their prison cell. She sees a prisoner with a knife in his chest. She gets the doctor. She opens the cell door for the doctor. The doctor puts his doctor's bag on the floor and in his dying moments, the prisoner points to something in the cell that allows the doctor to figure out who dunnit.

Solution:
Points to M.D. → Inmate #1500 on the bag

145

Name that Proverb

Primary
Junior
Intermediate
Senior

Group Size: 3 or 4 in a group

Time Line: 5 minutes

Equipment Needed: paper, pencil

Space Required: any convenient setting - clusters

Activity Description:

1. Group attempts to list at least 10 proverbs in the 5 minutes provided.
2. Reporter reads first half of proverb - rest of class completes the proverb (limit of 3 proverbs).
3. Next group reporter reads 3 different proverbs - whole class responds with 2nd half of proverb.
4. Continue until each group has reported.
5. Stump the class - get a point.

Sample:

A stitch in time...

Invitations To Dinner

Primary
Junior
Intermediate
Senior

Group Size: small groups of 3 or 4

Time Line: 5 minutes to write names, a few minutes for each person to discuss their answers.

Equipment Needed: none

Space Required: regular seating arrangements for the various co-operative groups

Activity Description:

1. Give each person approximately 5 minutes to write down 5 people that he/she would like to invite to dinner. These people may be historical, famous, T.V. personalities, political figures or from fiction.
2. During the sharing sessions, each person briefly states why he/she invited that particular person.
3. This is entertaining plus it is insightful regarding interests and hobbies of the people involved.

You're Invited

146

News Events Energizer

Group Size: 3-4

Time Line: 1-2 minutes

Equipment Needed: group only

Space Required: classroom

Activity Description:

1. Have students (in groups of 3-4) recall as many news events as they can, which have occurred over the past 24 hours.

Primary
Junior
Intermediate
Senior

Dictionary Game

Group Size: any size

Time Line: anywhere from 15 minutes to an hour

Equipment Needed: dictionary, paper, pens, blackboard

Space Required: a regular classroom, or any space

Activity Description:

1. Have students write invented definitions for words chosen by teacher on slips of paper, as well as adding the correct definitions.
2. Have them vote on the definition they think is the true definition.
3. Students get points for choosing the correct answer and fooling other students into choosing their definition.

Primary
Junior
Intermediate
Senior

ECLECTIC

147

12 Most Frequently Spoken Languages in the World

Primary
Junior
Intermediate
Senior

Group Size: small groups

Time Line: 7-8 minutes

Equipment Needed: overhead (possibly)

Activity Description:

1. Brainstorm among target group.
2. Report back to large group.

Languages Spoken By Most People

1. Mandarin
2. English
3. Hindi
4. Spanish
5. Russian
6. Arabic
7. Bengali
8. Portuguese
9. Malay - Indonesian
10. Japanese
11. French
12. German

(*World Almanac*, 1992)

What Was That You Said?

Primary
Junior
Intermediate
Senior

Group Size: whole class in groups

Time Line: 10 minutes

Equipment Needed: overhead or photocopies

Space Required: classroom

Activity Description:

1. Students read complicated phrases and attempt to translate them into well-known clichés and phrases.

See following pages.

148

What Was That You Said?

SEE IF YOU CAN TRANSLATE THESE WELL-KNOWN CLICHES AND PROVERBS:

Primary

Junior

Intermediate

Senior

1. Scintillate, scintillate, asteroid minikin.

2. Members of an avian species of identical plumage congregate.

3. Surveillance should precede saltation.

4. Pulchritude possesses solely cutaneous profundity.

5. It is fruitless to become lachrymose over precipitately departed lacteal fluid.

6. Freedom from encrustations of grime is continuous to rectitude.

7. The stylus is more potent than the claymore.

8. It is fruitless to attempt to indoctrinate a superannuated canine with innovative maneuvers.

9. Eschew the implementation of correction and vitiate the scion.

10. The temperature of the aqueous content of an unremittingly ogled saucepan does not reach 212 degrees Fahrenheit.

11. All articles that coruscate with resplendence are not truly auriferous.

12. Where there are visible vapours having their prevalence in ignited carbonaceous materials, there is conflagration.

13. Sorting on the part of mendicants must be interdicted.

14. A plethora of individuals with expertise in culinary techniques vitiates the potable concoction produced by steeping certain comestibles.

15. Eleemosynary deeds have their incipience intramurally.

16. Male cadavers are incapable of yielding testimony.

17. Individuals who make their abodes in vitreous edifices would be advised to refrain from catapulting petrous projectiles.

18. Neophyte's serendipity.

19. Exclusive dedication to necessitous chores without interlude of hedonist diversion renders John an unresponsive fellow.

20. A revolving lithic conglomerate accumulates no congeries of a small green bryophytic plant.

What's This Got To Do With Anything • Jim Craigen & Chris Ward
Kagan Publishing • 1 (800) 933-2667 • www.KaganOnline.com

What Was That You Said? (cont'd...)

Primary
Junior
Intermediate
Senior

21. The person presenting the ultimate cachinnation possesses thereby the optimal cachinnation.

22. Abstention from any alcatory undertakings precludes a potential escalation of a lucrative nature.

23. Missiles of ligneous or petrous consistency have the potential of fracturing my caseous structure, but appellations will eternally remain innocuous.

24. Persons of imbecilic mentality navigate in parameters which cherubic entities approach with trepidation.

25. Elementary sartorial techniques initially applied preclude repetitive similar action to a square of three.

★ ★

ANSWERS

1. Twinkle, twinkle, little star.
2. Birds of a feather flock together.
3. Look before you leap.
4. Beauty is only skin deep.
5. No use crying over spilt milk.
6. Cleanliness is next to godliness.
7. The pen is more powerful than the sword.
8. You can't teach an old dog new tricks.
9. Spare the rod and spoil the child.
10. A watched pot will never boil.
11. All that glitters is not gold.
12. Where there's smoke, there's fire.
13. Beggars can't be choosers.
14. Too many cooks spoil the broth.
15. Charity begins at home.
16. Dead men tell no tales.
17. People who live in glass houses shouldn't throw stones.
18. Beginner's luck.
19. All work and no play make Jack a dull boy.
20. A rolling stone gathers no moss.
21. He who laughs last laughs best.
22. Nothing ventured, nothing gained.
23. Sticks and stones can break my bones but words will never hurt me.
24. Fools rush in where angels fear to tread.
25. A stitch in time saves nine.

What's This Got To Do With Anything • Jim Craigen & Chris Ward
Kagan Publishing • 1 (800) 933-2667 • www.KaganOnline.com

Fruit Salad

Group Size: whole class

Time Line: 2+ minutes

Equipment Needed: none

Space Required: space for class to make a circle

Activity Description:

1. Brainstorm with class names of fruit (can be changed to fit any category or theme).
2. Choose 3-5 fruit names and call off around the circle assigning fruit names to students.
3. Director calls fruit name.
4. Each person must change places with another person of that name.
5. Director will also try to move into empty space.
6. Leftover person is the new director (caller) .
7. When category name is called, e.g. fruit, everyone changes places.

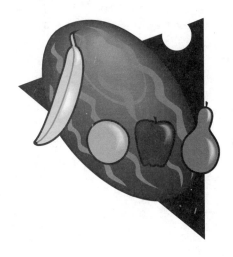

Who Is The Leader?

Group Size: any number

Time Line: 5 minutes

Equipment Needed: children

Space Required: room for the children to sit in a circle

Activity Description:

1. The children sit in a circle or at desks.
2. One person goes out.
3. Another person is the leader who does different actions in the circle.
4. The rest of the children in the circle follow along with the leader's actions.
5. The person who is hiding comes back to the circle and tries to guess who the leader is (i.e. leading the actions).

151

The Wave

Group Size: ten or more

Time Line: 5-15 minutes

Equipment Needed: active bodies only

Space Required:
open area large
enough to form
a circle

Activity Description:

1. The first person in the circle assumes some position of arms, legs, and body and holds it.
2. The second person copies and holds, then the third and so on until all members are holding the shape.
3. The next person in the circle can then try his/her own shape.
4. Try to move in sequence as quickly as possible to see the wave occur.

Honey, If You Love Me, Won't You Please, Please Smile

Group Size: large group

Time Line: this is up to you

Equipment Needed: none

Space Required: large open area

Activity Description:

1. Everyone stands in a circle.
2. One person stands in the centre.
3. Centre person picks someone in the circle, faces them, and says, "Honey, if you love me, won't you please, please smile".
4. The other person must respond by saying, "Honey, I love you; but I just can't smile".
5. This person cannot smile.
6. If this person smiles, he or she must become the centre person.

152

Interlocking Clap

Group Size: any number

Time Line: 10 minutes

Equipment Needed: nothing - just bodies, arms, hands

Space Required: round table (large) or large area of floor space

Activity Description:

1. Students lay on stomachs on floor, heads towards centre, shoulders touching.
2. Right arm crosses over left arm of person next to you.
4. Hands down on floor (flat).
5. Goal - to clap, in sequence, each hand all around the circle. (Same procedure can be adapted to sitting around a table or standing.)

Variation:
Clap out a specific rhythm - each person claps one beat of rhythm.

Seven Commands

Group Size: whole class divided into 2 groups

Time Line: 5 - 10 minutes

Equipment Needed: blindfold, object to be found

Space Required:
large open area

Activity Description:

1. Divide group into two groups.
2. One person from each group will be blindfolded.
3. Group has to direct blindfolded member to the hidden object using only these seven commands - up, down, right, left, forward, backwards, stop.

153

Peculiar Pencil

Primary
Junior
Intermediate
Senior

Group Size: 25

Time Line: 5 - 7 minutes

Equipment Needed: pencil or paint-brush

Space Required: classroom

Activity Description:

1. Arrange the class in a circle.
2. One person begins by taking a pencil and using it in a way that shows that the pencil has become something else.
3. The class must identify what the pencil has become.
4. Then the pencil is passed to the next person in the circle who must use it in a different way.
5. There can be no duplication, and the pencil should be passed around the circle several times.

That's A Great Idea!

Primary
Junior
Intermediate
Senior

Group Size: whole class activity or pairs or small groups

Time Line: 10 - 15 minutes

Equipment Needed: nothing

Space Required: classroom - desks pushed back

Activity Description:

1. Two volunteers go to the centre of the circle.
2. "A" suggests an activity, e.g. "Let's go for a walk". "B" must reply, "That's a great idea!" Support the improvisation with appropriate actions.
3. When "B" is ready, he/she suggests another activity in the spirit of the scene, e.g. "Lets pick some flowers".
4. "A" must reply now, "That's a great idea!" and continue the improvisation.
5. Allow the pattern to continue until a satisfactory ending.

What's This Got To Do With Anything • Jim Craigen & Chris Ward
Kagan Publishing • 1 (800) 933-2667 • www.KaganOnline.com

Pass The Squeeze, Grab The Keys

Group Size: 2 teams

Time Line: 15 - 20 minutes

Equipment Needed: 2 rows of chairs - one per person; set of keys; extra chair on end to put keys on; extra chair at other end for the "squeeze starter"

Space Required: large enough for 2 rows of chairs

Activity Description:

1. Students sit in 2 rows.
2. Two teams, facing in, holding hands with persons beside them, eyes closed, chairs touching.
4. Keys on end chair; at other end, sits person who is starting the squeeze (he/she is holding hands with the first person from each team).
5. The squeeze-starter begins the squeeze and it is passed down the line.
6. The last person who gets the squeeze, grabs the keys from chair
7. Team who gets keys first, gets the point.

Hint:
Practice the squeeze a few times before the game begins.

Freeze

Group Size: 20 - could be any size

Time Line: 10 - 15 minutes

Equipment Needed: nothing

Space Required: gym/large room

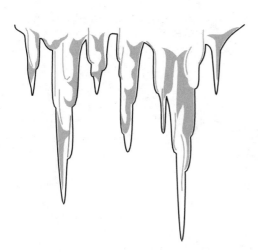

Activity Description:

1. A & B start a scene in the centre of the circle (any action).
2. Continue scene, teacher calls "freeze".
3. C steps in and takes A or B's space.
4. A new scene is created from the previous body positions *or* have kids spread out in room and act out any action.
5. Call "freeze"; students note their body position and begin a new activity. Continue "freeze".

155

Partner Pull-Up

Group Size: whole class working in pairs

Time Line: 5 minutes

Equipment Needed: nothing

Space Required: large open area

Activity Description:

1. In partners, students sit face to face, knees bent, toes touching one another and holding hands.
2. Together they try and pull themselves into standing position.
3. If successful, they can try the same activity working in groups of three's, four's, or five's.

Energizer

Group Size: individuals or small groups

Time Line: 3 minutes

Equipment Needed: pen and paper

Space Required: classroom

Activity Description:

1. Name as many 3-letter body parts as possible.
2. No unacceptable words!!

156

Got a Match?

Primary
Junior
Intermediate
Senior

Group Size: any size (for large groups colour code sets of quotes)

Time Line: 5 - 10 minutes

Equipment Needed: a set of quotations where each half is on a separate card. Laminated. Reversed masking tape on wall.
e.g. "CHANGE IS A PROCESS - "NOT AN EVENT"

Space Required: classroom

Activity Description:

1. Give each person 2 mismatched cards. The objective is to end up with one matched set.
2. Find the people who have same coloured cards.
3. Trade cards until everyone has a "matched" set, i.e. a complete quote.
4. Post on wall by pressing onto reversed masking tape.
5. *Variations:*
   Instead of quotations: try the term with definition; book titles split in half; title and author; vocabulary words; expressions e.g. Dec. 25 → Christmas, How are you? → I am fine; anything that is the theme of lesson and can be split.
   NEVER TRY TO TEACH A PIG TO SING... YOU WASTE YOUR TIME... AND, YOU ANNOY THE PIG!
6. For those who want competition, the team that finishes first wins/gets a prize.

All Rise Review

Primary
Junior
Intermediate
Senior

Group Size: whole class

Time Line: 5 minutes

Equipment Needed: class

Space Required: classroom

Activity Description:

1. When a class is dragging, get everyone to stand up.
2. Best during test review - when they answer a question group gets to sit down.
3. Conference is allowed - related to subject area being taught. If they talk when sitting, must stand back up.

157

What's This Got To Do With Anything • Jim Craigen & Chris Ward
Kagan Publishing • 1 (800) 933-2667 • www.KaganOnline.com

What Are You Doing?

Group Size: whole class

Time Line: until your group has completed the task

Equipment Needed: none

Space Required: area where group can get in a circle

Activity Description:

1. Group of 10 form a circle. One person begins by pantomiming a task, i.e. washing a car, painting a fence, etc.
2. The player on the right asks, "What are you doing?" The first player responds with a task different from what is actually being pantomimed, e.g. if the player is painting a fence, then he/she would respond with "Washing a dog."
3. The second player begins washing a dog and so on until the circle is completed.

Nine Square

Group Size: whole class

Time Line: 5 - 10 minutes

Equipment Needed: a writing surface (ground, blackboard, paper, etc.)

Space Required: classroom

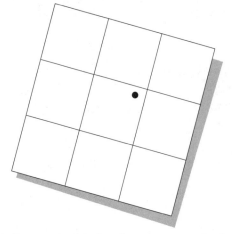

Activity Description:

1. This activity requires two people, one to guess the squares and one to be the pointer.
2. Construct a square with nine smaller squares inside.
3. Guesser leaves room, and a member of group chooses a square.
4. Guesser returns and the pointer points to squares and guesser chooses the correct one.

Method
The key or answer is given in the first point. On the first point the pointer simply points to that area within the smaller square that is indicative of the larger grid. Guesser must understand the game. If anyone within group understands the concept, he/she then becomes the guesser.

• *indicates top right hand corner square for first point*

What's This Got To Do With Anything • Jim Craigen & Chris Ward
Kagan Publishing • 1 (800) 933-2667 • www.KaganOnline.com

Pulse

Primary
Junior
Intermediate
Senior

Group Size: whole class

Time Line: 2 minutes

Equipment Needed: stop watch

Space Required: enough room to form a circle of people holding hands

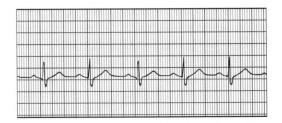

Activity Description:

1. Students form circle and hold hands. Teacher can be part of circle too.
2. One student, not part of the circle, is the timer.
3. Teacher says "Go" and at the same time gives a slight squeeze of his left hand.
4. As each student feels his right hand squeezed, s/he quickly squeezes his left hand to pass the pulse.
5. When the pulse arrives back at the teacher s/he says "Stop" to the time keeper.

Challenges:
beat last years time of 8 seconds, (outside force interdependence) - beat your own time - let pulse go the other way.

Looking At Things In New Ways

Primary
Junior
Intermediate
Senior

Group Size: any size

Time Line: 2 minutes

Equipment Needed: people

Space Required: nothing extra

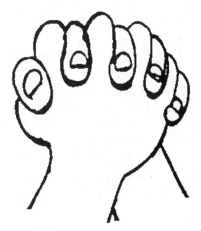

Activity Description:

1. Fold your hands together. How many have the right thumb on top? How many have the left thumb on top?
2. Now fold your hands with the other thumb on top. How does it feel? Awkward?
3. This is what it is like when we are trying to change or look at something in a new way.

Note:
Try the same thing with folding arms.

159

Musical Newspapers

Primary
Junior
Intermediate
Senior

Group Size: whole class

Time Line: 5 - 15 minutes

Equipment Needed: newspapers, tape and recorder (for music)

Space Required: open area (one half to three quarters of a classroom (desks moved over))

Activity Description:

1. Place 15 newspaper pages (single pages open) on floor.
2. Walk around room, when music stops (teacher controlled) everyone must get onto a newspaper.
3. Object - to save as many people as possible.
4. Reduce paper each time, until down to 1 or 2 pages.
5. Encourage students to think of ways to save the whole class (e.g. one foot on and hold hands so as not to fall).

Beat The Calculator

Primary
Junior
Intermediate
Senior

Group Size: - whole class or small groups

Time Line: 1 - 15 minutes

Equipment Needed: overhead projector, calculator

Space Required: classroom - whole class vs. calculator

Activity Description:

1. Teacher puts calculator on overhead projector so all students can see calculator on screen.
2. Teacher keys in an equation (i.e. 10 + 5 =   ).
3. If the students yell out the answer before the teacher pushes the equal sign, then the students get a point.
4. If the teacher pushes the equal sign before the students yell out the answer, then the calculator gets a point.
5. Students are not allowed to use calculators. Students usually beat the calculator and they feel great!

160

Let's Get Physical

Group Size: whole class

Time Line: 2 minutes

Equipment Needed: none

Space Required: 4 - 5 square feet per person

Activity Description:

1. A brief exercise routine.
2. Hands above head and stretch.
3. Hands down.
4. Arms out.
5. Swing back and forth, feet remain fixed on floor.
6. Repeat "X" number of times (1 - 4).
7. Shake hands only from wrist.
8. Relax.
9. Return to seats.

Primary
Junior
Intermediate
Senior

What If..?

Group Size: whole class or groups

Time Line: 5 - 6 minutes

Equipment Needed: none

Space Required: classroom

Activity Description:

1. Teacher gives a starter statement - "What if you had an eye on the end of your index finger..."
2. In turn students reply.
3. Responses may not be repeated. However, students may pass if they cannot think of an idea.
4. Responses are to be given in rapid succession.

Primary
Junior
Intermediate
Senior

161

Bunny, Elephant, Palm Tree

Primary
Junior
Intermediate
Senior

Group Size: 10 and up

Time Line: 5 minutes

Equipment Needed: none

Space Required: large open space

Activity Description:

1. Form a large circle with one person standing in the middle as "it". The person in the centre first demonstrates positions for people to take when he/she calls out either bunny, elephant or palm tree.
2. The person in the centre then twirls around and points his/her finger at one of the people in the circle and shouts either "bunny" or "elephant" or "palm tree".
3. The person pointed to and the two people on either side take the appropriate positions with their bodies. If someone messes up, they're the new "it".

Bunny: middle person makes paws up using both hands. Right hand side person extends left arm up (close to middle person to form ear); left hand side person extends right arm up (close to middle person to form ear).

Elephant: middle person forms trunk using both arms, right person uses both arms in a circular position to form the ear; left person uses both arms in a circular position to form other ear.

Palm tree: middle person stands straight with both arms extended straight over head; right person uses both arms and bends away to the right; left person uses both arms and bends away to the left.

Fitness Break

Primary
Junior
Intermediate
Senior

Group Size: whole class

Time Line: 5 minutes (open)

Equipment Needed: nothing

Space Required: minimum

Activity Description:

1. In the middle of the lesson or when you think you need it, do a fitness break, where students can do a mini-aerobic lesson. This includes stretching, hopping, walking, jumping jacks, push-ups.
3. Do simple things that the teacher is comfortable with. It is a simple thing but it seems to work.

What's This Got To Do With Anything • Jim Craigen & Chris Ward
Kagan Publishing • 1 (800) 933-2667 • www.KaganOnline.com

Fun Fridays

Group Size: whole class

Time Line: last 15 - 20 minutes of class

Equipment Needed: crossword, game of your choice

Space Required: classroom

Activity Description:

1. The last few minutes of a Friday class is a "Fun Friday".
2. Teacher gives a crossword or a word-search or plays a game or something fun.
3. I have found the students look forward to it, and my attendance on Fridays has improved 200%.

Vocabulary Bee

Group Size: groups of 4 - 5

Time Line: 1 - 2 minutes (maximum)

Equipment Needed: pencil and paper

Space Required: group tables

Activity Description:

1. Work with your home group.
2. Teacher/student choose a topic.
3. Choose 1 - 5 letters from the alphabet.
4. In home groups, brainstorm words for a topic that begin with any of the letters.
5. When time is finished begin with any group. Volunteer gives one word. If another group has that word - no point given. If only that group has this word - point scored.
6. Tally points put on thermometer chart.

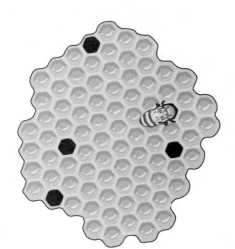

163

Tongue Twisters

Group Size: class divided into 3's

Time Line: 1 minute or less, (30 seconds or 20 seconds per person)

Equipment Needed: none

Space Required: none

Activity Description:

1. In a group of three - 1 timer, 1 reciter and 1 counter.
2. Try to say a tongue twister as many times as you can.
3. Each person gets one attempt.

Knots

Group Size: any uneven number of people

Time Line: 15 minutes

Equipment Needed: people

Space Required: depends on the size of the group

Activity Description:

1. Have people stand in a circle.
2. Ask all to reach out and grab two other hands (you cannot have both hands of one person, and you cannot have the hand of persons on each side of you).
3. One person must leave right arm out and one person must leave left arm out.
4. Now, untangle so that all are standing in a line - AND DON'T LET GO!

What's This Got To Do With Anything • Jim Craigen & Chris Ward
Kagan Publishing • 1 (800) 933-2667 • www.KaganOnline.com

Hagoo

Group Size: whole class in 2 groups

Time Line: 10 - 15 minutes or longer if desired

Equipment Needed: none

Space Required: open area in the classroom

Activity Description:

1. Divide the class into two lines facing each other.
2. First person from Line "A" steps forward and then walks sideways slowly all along the front of Line"B."
3. The people in line "B" must try to make this person walking slowly in front of them laugh.
4. If the person does laugh they must join line "B".
5. If the person is successful and does not laugh they return to the end of their own line.
6. Line "B" does the same.
7. The game ends when everybody has had a turn.

One To Ten

Group Size: whole class

Time Line: 5 minutes

Equipment Needed: none

Space Required: classroom

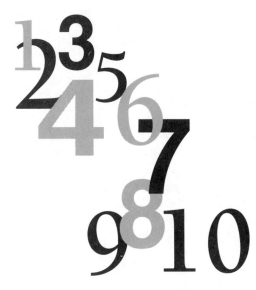

Activity Description:

1. The students all stand up at their desks.
2. They then start the count.
3. They may say just one number, like "one" or they can say two numbers, "one, two".
4. The next must say either the next or the next two numbers on the way to counting to "ten".
5. If a student gets stuck with saying "ten" he/she must sit down.
6. The count then starts again.
7. The last student left standing gets the prize. Any age loves it! My grade 9's begged to play it every day.

Variation:
(higher numbers, multiples of numbers or numbers in another language).

165

Shoe Scramble

Group Size: whole class

Time Line: 10 - 20 minutes

Equipment Needed: everyone has to wear shoes

Space Required: classroom or gym (large enough for a class to make a circle)

Activity Description:

1. Form a circle with your classmates.
2. Each person in the circle must take off *one* shoe and place it in the middle.
3. When this has been done, everyone must join hands.
4. Then, without letting go of the hands, each person must pick one shoe other than their own, find the owner of the shoe, and return it to him or her.
5. *Remember:* Hands must be held at all times. It will soon be very clear why this needs to be a co-operative activity.

Object Hunt

Group Size: whole class

Time Line: 5 minutes

Equipment Needed: a paper clip or any object

Space Required: classroom

Activity Description:

1. As all eyes are hidden - one person puts a paper clip in a prominent place.
2. Everyone walks around - no talking allowed - looking.
3. When they find it they **must** look in 3 more places before sitting down in order not to disclose the hiding place.
4. When all are seated someone is chosen to disclose the hiding place.
5. This may also be done in pairs.

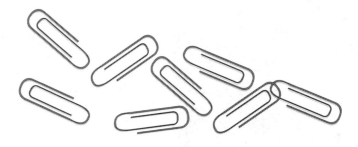

What's This Got To Do With Anything • Jim Craigen & Chris Ward
Kagan Publishing • 1 (800) 933-2667 • www.KaganOnline.com

Wink Murder

Primary
Junior
Intermediate
Senior

Group Size: whole class

Time Line: 5 - 10 minutes

Equipment Needed: none

Space Required: classroom - clear desks aside

Activity Description:

1. Wink Murder - Students in a sitting circle facing all members.
2. Teacher taps one student, while all others have eyes closed, to be the murderer.
3. Murderer kills victims by winking at them - where upon the victim dramatically "dies". Others guess who the murderer is.

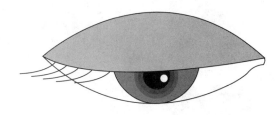

Club Med In The Classroom

Primary
Junior
Intermediate
Senior

Group Size: whole class

Time Line: 5 minutes

Equipment Needed: tape recorder or C.D. player and copy of "Hands Up, Baby, Hands Up".

Space Required: classroom

Activity Description:

1. Each team has 1 minute to come up with 5 upper body exercises that can be done while seated, to music.
2. Assign roles - time keeper, recorder, demonstrator, etc.
3. The teacher then puts on the music and the demonstrator from each team leads the class in "quality daily P.E." as an energizer.

167

Jump And Yell

Primary
Junior
Intermediate
Senior

Group Size: whole class

Time Line: short period of time

Equipment Needed: none

Space Required: enough room for students to jump

Activity Description:

1. Facilitator calls out a category, and at the count of three, students simultaneously jump, as high as they can and yell as loud as they can, their answer.
2. Then they freeze silently upon landing until next category is called. (Example of categories: favourite colour, dream car, detested food, favourite rock group.)

Balloon Issues

Primary
Junior
Intermediate
Senior

Group Size: whole class (may divide into smaller groups)

Time Line: 10 minutes

Equipment Needed: balloons with issues or topics written on them

Space Required: classroom area with slight rearrangement of desks

Activity Description:

1. Students sit in seats in a circle facing each other and must keep the balloons in the air by batting them around.
2. When a balloon hits the ground in the circle the last person to touch it must comment on the issue or answer the question.
3. Then the balloons are started again.
4. Each student may pass once or twice.

What's This Got To Do With Anything • Jim Craigen & Chris Ward
Kagan Publishing • 1 (800) 933-2667 • www.KaganOnline.com

Restructuring Words

Group Size: groups of 3 to 5

Time Line: 3 minutes

Equipment Needed: 1 multi-syllabic word

Space Required: classroom

Activity Description:

1. Challenge groups to find as many smaller words as they can within the larger word.
2. Letters may be rearranged.
3. Announce time limit.
4. Total number of words generated by the class can be posted.
5. Try to beat this number the next time.

Antidisestablishmentarianism

Group Juggling

Group Size: 8 - 10 students

Time Line: 8 - 10 minutes

Equipment Needed: nerf balls or koosh balls

Space Required: classroom

Activity Description:

1. Begin in a circle.
2. Ball is passed to someone who is not directly beside a student.
3. Students are to remember who they passed the ball to.
4. Each student touches the ball once.
5. The students then are to remember the pattern and repeat it exactly without talking to each other.
6. Then the teacher can introduce 2nd or 3rd ball to achieve "Group Juggling".

169

Balloon Float

Group Size: groups of 5 to 8 people

Time Line: 5 minutes

Equipment Needed: a balloon for each group

Space Required: enough for groups to form circles

Activity Description:

1. Groups of students form circles facing inward, hands joined.
2. The object is to keep the balloon up in the air without disconnecting hands.
3. Students won't mind holding hands this way (hopefully).
4. The class may discuss later what made the groups successful (i.e. co-operation).

Team Tag

Group Size: whole class in groups of 2, 3 or 4

Time Line: 10 minutes

Equipment Needed: none

Space Required: gym/outdoors

Activity Description:

1. Class gets into groups of 2, 3 or 4.
2. One group is "it" and must remain together as must the other groups.
3. Once the group has tagged another group, the tagged group becomes "it".
4. *Note:* the group that works best together will get tagged the least.

What's This Got To Do With Anything • Jim Craigen & Chris Ward
Kagan Publishing • 1 (800) 933-2667 • www.KaganOnline.com

Creative Brainstorming

Group Size: groups of 2

Time Line: 2 - 5 minutes

Equipment Needed: may want
paper/pen

Space Required: classroom-room for
pairs to work

Activity Description:

1. With your partner explain how your life
would change if you could "fly" or if you
were placed in any other hypothetical
situation.
2. These may or may not be shared with
the class.

Primary
Junior
Intermediate
Senior

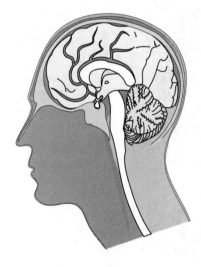

Same And Different

Group Size: 6 or more

Time Line: 10 minutes

Equipment Needed: chairs for everyone
except one person

Space Required: large clear area, chairs
in circle

Activity Description:

1. All students sit in chairs.
2. Teacher asks all students wearing something similar to stand and exchange
seats.
3. Teacher sits in a chair so one student is
left standing.
4. That student points out something similar and it begins again (e.g. white socks,
jeans, shirt with collar).
5. Point out everyone has similarities and
differences with each other.

Primary
Junior
Intermediate
Senior

171

I Like People

Primary
Junior
Intermediate
Senior

Group Size: whole class

Time Line: 15 minutes

Equipment Needed: chairs in a circle

Space Required: large open space

Activity Description:

1. The whole class sits in circle.
2. There is one less chair than number of people.
3. One person who has no chair stands in middle of circle while everyone else is in a chair.
4. That person says, "I like people and I especially like people who e.g. wear glasses". All people who wear glasses get up and find an empty chair (including person in the middle).
5. Left over person goes to centre and calls, "I like people and I especially like people who whatever - e.g. have a dog, have blue eyes, etc.
6. Game continues.

Snowball Game

Primary
Junior
Intermediate
Senior

Group Size: whole class

Time Line: 3 - 5 minutes

Equipment Needed: paper (good for recycling)

Space Required: classroom

Activity Description:

1. Students write down 1 thing they know or have learned about a subject on a small piece of paper.
2. Crunch up the paper when finished writing.
3. Begin to toss the papers around the room.
4. As papers are caught, open them, read them, crunch them up again and continue tossing them.
5. The game can go on as long as you like.

172

Creative Thinking Energizers

Group Size: groups of 3 or 4 students

Time Line: 5 to 7 minutes approximately, depending on group

Equipment Needed: paper, pencil

Space Required: classroom groupings of 3 or 4

Activity Description:

1. Either one question or a series of questions in envelopes are given to students. (e.g. Name 20 soft, blue things etc.)
2. They are given 5 to 7 minutes to think of creative responses.
3. This activity is perfect at the start of the day or just after lunch, to get the brains working again.
4. After the question(s) has/have been brainstormed, the answers are presented to the class.
5. There can be a Presenter, Writer, Timekeeper and Encourager.

Television Trivia

Group Size: whole class

Time Line: 5 - 15 minutes

Equipment Needed: bells, small musical instruments, etc. - one per group; info cards with answers on them

Space Required: classroom - break class into pairs or appropriate sized teams

Activity Description:

1. The teacher or game host reads a card.
2. The group pairs or teams can huddle and discuss possible answers.
3. When a team knows the answer, they use their sound effect (or gesture) to signal to host and class.
4. They tell class and if correct, gain points.
5. Use game cards with popular T.V. show clues on them. You can emphasize whatever you want: plot, character studies, setting, simple math, etc.

173

Frozen Feelings

Primary
Junior
Intermediate
Senior

Group Size: groups of 5

Time Line: whatever time you have

Equipment Needed: none

Space Required: classroom

Activity Description:

1. One person stands, thinks of an emotion (or choses one from a list) he/she wishes to portray and freezes it on his/her face. (This would be best to do after having taught tableaux in drama.)
2. 1 minute for rest to say and write words to describe frozen person's feelings.
3. Person frozen must have a focal point and must try to *not break* concentration during one minute.
4. Have each person take a turn.
5. This builds vocabulary, helps special students to read people's feelings by observing faces and lastly, helps them to stay completely concentrated on something for a time limit.

Perker Upper

Primary
Junior
Intermediate
Senior

Group Size: small groups

Time Line: 3 minutes - 1 to write "perk", 2 to exchange and guess

Equipment Needed: paper and pen/pencil, groups with 3 or 4 individuals per group

Space Required: enough for groups

Activity Description:

1. Pair groups.
2. In own group, students write down something they like about someone else in the other partner group.
3. Each member in group A picks 1 member of group B and vice versa.
4. People in your own group know who others in your group picked. This avoids duplication.
5. People in group receiving compliments have to guess which compliment applies to whom, and who wrote it.

174

Creative Uses

Primary
Junior
Intermediate
Senior

Group Size: whole class (30) or half class (15), depending on time allotted

Time Line: 10 minutes

Equipment Needed: the object you choose - try to use an object that will lend itself to many uses

Space Required: spot where everyone will be able to see the person with the object

Activity Description:

1. Teacher or students choose an object.
2. Each person has a few seconds (5 to 10) to think of, and demonstrate a use for the object, other then what it is normally used for - i.e. a ruler used as a:
   i) razor
   ii) cane
   iii) music conductor's stick.
3. Allow all students an opportunity with the object.
4. Encourage, but do not force students to participate.

Estimation

Primary
Junior
Intermediate
Senior

Group Size: whole class

Time Line: 2 - 3 minutes

Equipment Needed: textbook

Space Required: desktop

Activity Description:

1. With any book or text, identify a common page.
2. Try to open your text to the exact page or as close to it as possible.
3. Can give a prize, but not necessary.

175

See last page for ordering info

Index